Presented To:

From:

Date:

RIGHTLY DIVIDING
THE WORD

Books by Ira L. Milligan

Understanding the Dreams You Dream (Revised): Biblical Keys for Hearing God's Voice in the Night

Understanding the Dreams You Dream Vol. II: Every Dreamer's Handbook

The Scorpion Within: Revealing the Eight Demonic Roots of Sin

AVAILABLE FROM DESTINY IMAGE PUBLISHERS

RIGHTLY DIVIDING THE WORD

UNLOCKING THE HIDDEN MYSTERIES OF THE BIBLE

IRA L. MILLIGAN

 Emphasis within Scripture quotations is the author's own. Please note that Destiny Image's publishing style capitalizes certain pronouns in Scripture that refer to the Father, Son, and Holy Spirit, and may differ from some publishers' styles. Take note that the name satan and related names are not capitalized. We choose not to acknowledge him, even to the point of violating grammatical rules.

DESTINY IMAGE® PUBLISHERS, INC.
P.O. Box 310, Shippensburg, PA 17257-0310
"Promoting Inspired Lives."

This book and all other Destiny Image, Revival Press, MercyPlace, Fresh Bread, Destiny Image Fiction, and Treasure House books are available at Christian bookstores and distributors worldwide.

For a U.S. bookstore nearest you, call 1-800-722-6774.
For more information on foreign distributors, call 717-532-3040.
Reach us on the Internet: www.destinyimage.com.

ISBN 13 TP: 978-0-7684-3903-8

ISBN 13 Ebook: 978-0-7684-8956-9

For Worldwide Distribution, Printed in the U.S.A.
1 2 3 4 5 6 / 24 23 22 21

Be diligent to present yourself approved to God, a worker who does not need to be ashamed, ***rightly dividing the word of truth*** (2 Timothy 2:15 NKJV).

Contents

Part I

God's Word

Part II

A Perfect Heart

PART I

GOD'S WORD

In the beginning was the Word, and the Word was with God, and the Word was God. The same was in the beginning with God. All things were made by Him; and without Him was not any thing made that was made (John 1:1-3).

Introduction

God's Word Is His Bond

In the beginning was the Word, and the Word was with God, and ***the Word was God****....And the* ***Word was made flesh****, and dwelt among us...* (John 1:1,14).

Jesus is the Word. He is Lord, and He is the head of His Body, the Church. In these last days there is a growing move to discredit His lordship. This is being accomplished by ignoring or denying His Word. Because Jesus ***is*** the Word of God, to ignore or deny its authority is to dethrone Christ. If God's Word isn't Lord in our church, then Jesus isn't Lord in our church. Likewise, if His Word isn't the first, the foremost, and the final authority in our own personal lives, then He isn't our Lord either. For this reason, it is of utmost importance that we know and understand His Word.

Christians know that at the name of Jesus every knee shall bow and every tongue shall confess that Jesus Christ is Lord, and even the demons are subject to us through the power of His name, yet God has exalted His Word even above His name! (See Philippians 2:10-11 and Luke 10:17.)

> *I will worship toward Thy holy temple, and praise Thy name for Thy lovingkindness and for Thy truth:* ***for Thou hast magnified Thy word above all Thy name*** (Psalm 138:2).

And we should magnify our word, too! This is of necessity. Our name can never be greater than our word. If we fail to keep our word, we will lose our reputation as a faithful messenger. As ministers of the Gospel, nothing could be more disastrous. Likewise, when we fail to keep His Word, we bring a reproach upon His name and ours, because we are His representatives. As His ambassadors, we are given full authority to minister His Word, Spirit, and power (see 1 Cor. 2:4; Luke 10:19). An irresponsible steward who uses this authority selfishly or carelessly brings an evil reproach upon His name. Because God is jealous of His glory and carefully guards His reputation, He will not hold an unfaithful steward guiltless.

> *A good name is rather to be chosen than great riches, and loving favor rather than silver and gold* (Proverbs 22:1).

> *[After David sinned, the Lord sent him word, saying,] because by this deed thou hast given great occasion to the enemies of the Lord to blaspheme, the child also that is born unto thee shall surely die* (2 Samuel 12:14).

> *And upon a set day Herod, arrayed in royal apparel, sat upon his throne, and made an oration unto them. And the people gave a shout, saying, It is the voice of a god, and not of a man. And immediately the angel of the Lord smote him, because he gave not God the glory: and he was eaten of worms, and gave up the ghost* (Acts 12:21-23).

God's Word is His bond. He is so faithful to His Word that He still keeps it even when He's angry.

> *And the Lord said unto Moses, I have seen this people, and, behold, it is a stiff-necked people: Now therefore let Me alone, that*

> *My wrath may wax hot against them, and that I may consume them: and I will make of thee a great nation. And Moses besought the Lord his God, and said, Lord, why doth Thy wrath wax hot against Thy people, which Thou hast brought forth out of the land of Egypt with great power, and with a mighty hand?* ***Wherefore should the Egyptians speak, and say, For mischief did He bring them out, to slay them in the mountains, and to consume them from the face of the earth?*** *Turn from Thy fierce wrath, and repent of this evil against Thy people. Remember Abraham, Isaac, and Israel, Thy servants,* ***to whom Thou swarest by Thine own self,*** *and said unto them, I will multiply your seed as the stars of heaven, and all this land that I have spoken of will I give unto your seed, and they shall inherit it for ever. And the Lord repented of the evil which He thought to do unto His people* (Exodus 32:9-14).

Take note that Moses pointed out if God didn't do what He promised, even though Israel failed to meet His conditions, He was going to lose face. The Egyptians simply wouldn't understand. They would see only that the Israelites' God had failed to keep His promise! Moses correctly saw that God would lose face regardless of whose fault it was. So often it's that way, and God knows it. Therefore, to preserve His glory, His stated policy is:

> *For Mine own sake, even for Mine own sake, will I do it: for how should My name be polluted?* ***and I will not give My glory unto another*** (Isaiah 48:11).

If we dishonor Him or take His glory, sooner or later we are doomed to failure and humiliation. God will not defend our reputation, only His! So, if we steal His glory or bring dishonor on His name, we're in serious trouble.[1]

The best way to avoid trouble is to hide His Word in our hearts so that we won't sin against Him (see Ps. 119:7). There are many advantages of having His Word abiding within. Jesus said, *"If ye abide in Me, and My words abide in you, ye shall ask what ye will, and it shall be done unto you"* (John 15:7).

> *The law of the Lord is perfect, converting the soul: the testimony of the Lord is sure, making wise the simple. The statutes of the Lord are right, rejoicing the heart: the commandment of the Lord is pure, enlightening the eyes. The fear of the Lord is clean, enduring for ever: the judgments of the Lord are true and righteous altogether. More to be desired are they than gold, yea, than much fine gold: sweeter also than honey and the honeycomb. Moreover by them is Thy servant warned:* ***and in keeping of them there is great reward*** (Psalm 19:7-11).

> *...There is a natural body, and there is a spiritual body.... Howbeit that was not first which is spiritual, but that which is natural; and afterward that which is spiritual* (1 Corinthians 15:44,46).

Endnote

1. Adapted from Ira Milligan, *Understanding the Dreams You Dream, Vol. II* (Servant Ministries, Inc., 2000), 118-120.

LESSON ONE

FIRST THE NATURAL, THEN THE SPIRITUAL

Study to shew thyself approved unto God, a workman that needeth not to be ashamed, ***rightly dividing the word of truth*** (2 Timothy 2:15).

There are two primary divisions of the Word of God—the *natural* and the *spiritual.* Another way of stating this is that first the natural, historical events happened, and then the spiritual purposes and meanings of those events were revealed and fulfilled. Thus the *natural* division, which is commonly known as the *literal* interpretation, corresponds to the historical facts recorded in the Bible. The *spiritual* division corresponds to the spiritual interpretation and fulfillment in the person of Christ and His Church. The literal meaning is quite easy to see and understand, but the truth contained in the spiritual revelation is often well hidden.

For My thoughts are not your thoughts, neither are your ways My ways, saith the Lord. For as the heavens are higher than the earth, so are My ways higher than your ways, and My thoughts than your thoughts (Isaiah 55:8-9).

Isaiah said that God doesn't think like we do. For that reason, we cannot casually read His Word and still understand what He meant when He wrote it. Jesus said that His heavenly Father, "*...hid these things from the wise and prudent, and...revealed them unto babes...*" (Luke 10:21). One cannot find something that God hid without God Himself revealing His hiding place. John said, *"A man can receive nothing, except it be given him from heaven"* (John 3:27). Therefore, before beginning a search for His well-hidden, spiritual treasures, it's wise to take time out and pray for the *"spirit of wisdom and revelation"* (Eph. 1:17) to get His help in finding the truth.

> *Open Thou mine eyes, that I may behold wondrous things out of Thy law* (Psalm 119:18).

The Scriptures were written by men under the inspiration of the Holy Spirit (see 2 Tim. 3:16). Even when they simply recorded historical events, there was a spiritual purpose in what they wrote. Only those facts and events that were relevant to the spiritual truth that God wanted us to receive were recorded. This explains why there are so many unanswered questions about what *is* recorded.

For example, many people wonder where Cain's bride came from (see Gen. 4:17). Whose daughter was she? God didn't bother telling us because it wouldn't have revealed anything spiritually important. The "rest of the story" wouldn't teach us anything of eternal value, so He left it out. God didn't write His Word to satisfy our curiosity. Instead it contains *"all things that pertain unto life and godliness"* (2 Pet. 1:3). Every word is important, because every word contains eternal truth.

All Scripture is given by inspiration of God, and is profitable for doctrine, for reproof, for correction, for instruction in righteousness (see 2 Tim. 3:16).

But the natural man receiveth not the things of the Spirit of God: for they are foolishness unto him: neither can he know them, because they are spiritually discerned (1 Corinthians 2:14).

Because the Word is divinely inspired and its primary purpose is to reveal spiritual truth, carnal-minded people cannot understand it. When "learned" people take God's Word and attempt to "fill in the blanks," they make a grievous error. Likewise, those who stubbornly refuse to incorporate what He *did* write into their doctrinal understanding, or who leave parts out for convenience sake, make an equally disastrous mistake.

For I testify unto every man that hears the words of the prophecy of this book, If any man shall add unto these things, God shall add unto him the plagues that are written in this book: And if any man shall take away from the words of the book of this prophecy, God shall take away his part out of the book of life, and out of the holy city, and from the things which are written in this book (Revelation 22:18-19).

One of God's favorite tactics to hide truth is to place it in plain sight, but disguise it as something other than what it is. Almost all spiritual truth is first clothed with a natural disguise. When we look behind the natural covering, we find the naked truth!

Howbeit that was not first which is spiritual, but that which is natural; and afterward that which is spiritual (1 Corinthians 15:46).

An example of this is Moses' Law. The Law was a natural form of the truth, which was ordained to life, but the Jews didn't understand it (see Rom. 2:20; 7:10). They were unable to separate the natural commandments from the spiritual truths hidden within; therefore, the Law became death unto them.

Paul said that the letter of the Law kills, but the Spirit gives life (see 2 Cor. 3:6). The natural husk must be removed from the grain before it is edible. All the carnal ordinances and commandments of the Law contain spiritual truth. These truths are *"life unto those that find them, and health to all their flesh"* (Prov. 4:22).

> *For we know that* ***the law is spiritual:*** *but I am carnal, sold under sin* (Romans 7:14).

Although Paul said the Law is spiritual, the carnal commandments that contain it are not. As in the example of the aforementioned grain, one has to remove the outer, natural covering of the Law before the spiritual content is revealed. John said, *"the Word* [the Law and the prophets] *was made flesh..."* (John 1:14). Thus Jesus' flesh was the living expression of the natural ordinances and commands of the Law. He demonstrated the spirit of the Law rather than the letter of the Law. One has to look beyond His flesh (the outer covering) and see His heart to behold the Spiritual truth He embodied, which the Jews were unable to do. They only saw the outer, natural covering (see Matt. 13:53-57).

Jesus said, *"It is the Spirit who gives life;* ***the flesh profits nothing:*** *the words that I speak to you are spirit, and they are life"* (John 6:63 NKJV).

One example of using the Law correctly is found in First Corinthians 9:7-14. In the Law Moses wrote, *"Thou shalt not muzzle the ox when he treadeth out the corn"* (Deut. 25:4). But Paul quoted this law and then asked:

> *..."Is it oxen God is concerned about? Or does He say it altogether for our sakes?...If we have sown spiritual things for you, is it a great thing if we reap your material things?...So the Lord*

has commanded that those who preach the gospel should live from the gospel" (1 Corinthians 9:9-11,14 NKJV).

Here we see that Paul looked at the natural process of feeding oxen while they worked and applied that principle to the support of God's laborers. The oxen symbolized God's ministers. So the *letter* of the Law appeared to show concern for oxen, but the *spirit* of the Law revealed God's concern for His laborers.

This simple truth should be kept in mind when other Scriptures about oxen are read. By taking the truths revealed in the New Testament by Jesus and the apostles, and using them as keys to unlock the mysteries of the Old Testament, there is a wealth of information available to those who patiently search them out. For example, we can use what we just learned about oxen to open many more Scriptures about God's laborers.

When David attempted to take the ark of God from Abinadab's house to Jerusalem, he placed it on an ox-drawn cart. But as they went toward Jerusalem, the oxen stumbled. When they did, one of the men named Uzza put forth his hand to steady the ark and God killed him. When one substitutes ministers for oxen, and learns the meanings of Abinadab and Uzza's names, the spiritual meaning hidden in this story comes to light (see 1 Chron. 13:7-10).

Abinadab means "the father of generosity," and *Uzza* means "strength" (of man).[1] Although God expects His laborers to be supported by His children's generous giving, ministers make a big mistake (stumble) when they draw on the sheep's generosity and substitute the "strength" of people (money) for God's proper order. God may use people's ingenuity and wealth at times, but only if He chooses to do so, and then only as He directs!

Some teachers simply apply the Law as it is, without even making an attempt at obtaining the spiritual meaning. Paul said these people are, *"Desiring to be teachers of the law; understanding neither what they say, nor whereof they affirm"* (1 Tim. 1:7). When they do this, they destroy themselves and those who follow them.

Jesus died to free us from the Law. When preachers put God's flock back under it, they bring a curse upon themselves. When certain Jews came to Galatia and told Paul's converts they had to keep Moses' Law and be circumcised to be saved, Paul responded with a scathing rebuke:

> *But though we, or an angel from heaven, preach any other gospel unto you than that which we have preached unto you, let him be accursed. As we said before, so say I now again, If any man preach any other gospel unto you...let him be accursed* (Galatians 1:8-9).

A good example of the *incorrect* use of the Law is when pastors tell their flocks that the Bible says women aren't allowed to wear pants. Indeed, Moses' Law says that a *"woman shall not wear that which pertains unto a man, neither shall a man put on a woman's garment: for all that do so are abomination unto the Lord thy God"* (Deut. 22:5), but it also says, *"...the Lord sees not as man sees; for man looks on the outward appearance, but the Lord looks on the heart"* (1 Sam. 16:7). Paul referred to the spiritual meaning of Moses' commandment in First Corinthians:

> *Know ye not that the unrighteous shall not inherit the kingdom of God? Be not deceived: neither fornicators, nor idolaters, nor adulterers,* ***nor effeminate,*** *nor abusers of themselves with mankind* (1 Corinthians 6:9).

Masculine women and *effeminate* men are an abomination to God. They have corrupted God's design. God wants men to be men and women to be women. It's not our outside clothes, but the inner spiritual clothing we wear that God cares about. His dress code is found in Romans 13:14, *"But put ye on the Lord Jesus Christ, and make not provision for the flesh, to fulfill the lusts thereof."* Those who are clothed with the Spirit of Christ are well-dressed as far as God is concerned. Those who are clothed with their own works are naked before Him, *"...for by the works of the law shall no flesh be justified"* (Gal. 2:16).

The question of what part of the natural Law that still applies to the Church today was answered once and for all at the conference at Jerusalem in Acts chapter 15. When *"certain men which came down* [to Antioch] *from Judaea taught the brethren, and said, Except ye be circumcised after the manner of Moses, ye cannot be saved"* (Acts 15:1), the church sent Paul and Barnabas to the apostles in Jerusalem. If we don't want to put ourselves under the curse of Galatians 1:8-9, we should carefully consider the decision the apostles came up with at that time.

> *And they wrote letters...unto the brethren which are of the Gentiles....Forasmuch as we have heard, that certain which went out from us have troubled you with words, subverting your souls, saying, Ye must be circumcised, and keep the law: to whom we gave no such commandment: It seemed good unto us, being assembled with one accord, to send chosen men unto you with our beloved Barnabas and Paul...* ***For it seemed good to the Holy Ghost, and to us, to lay upon you no greater burden than these necessary things****; That ye abstain from meats offered to idols, and from blood, and from things strangled, and from fornication: from which if ye keep yourselves, ye shall do well...* (Acts 15:23-29).

Jesus satisfied the righteous requirements of the Law, fulfilling them in His life and death. In the process, He, *"blott*[ed] *out the handwriting of ordinances that was against us, which was contrary to us, and took it out of the way, nailing it to His cross"* (Col. 2:14). Through faith in the finished work of Christ, we *"are not under the law, but under grace....For the law of the Spirit of life in Christ Jesus hath made me free from the law of sin and death"* (Rom. 6:14; 8:2).

Law and grace won't mix. In fact, the Law itself forbids mingling the two. God said, *"...thou shalt not sow thy field with mingled seed...,"* and Jesus said, *"...the seed is the word of God"* (Lev. 19:19; Luke 8:11). Every seed brings forth after its own kind. When Law seed is sown into a person's heart, the fruit it bears is bondage and death; conversely, when God's grace is planted, it brings forth life and peace (see Rom. 8:6).

Whatsoever people sow, *that* shall they also reap. The natural seed is temporary; the spiritual is eternal. The natural seed is only a reflection of the supernatural. It is but a brief, shadowy image of the eternal truth it conveys. The spiritual reveals and fulfills the dark, prophetic image, which is dimly reflected by the Law.

> *For now we see in a mirror, dimly, but then face to face. Now I know in part, but then I shall know just as I also am known* (1 Corinthians 13:12 NKJV).

ASSIGNMENT: LESSON ONE

1. Show the spiritual meaning of Exodus 15:23-25.
2. Name the two primary divisions of the Word.
3. Which division corresponds to the Law, and which one corresponds to grace?
4. Which natural commandments and ordinances are we still required to obey?
5. Has the whole Law been, "done away with," as some teach?

6. A. What parts of the *spirit* of the Law are we supposed to keep?

   B. How?

7. Reading assignment: Genesis chapter 37 and chapters 39 through 45.

Endnote

1. J.B. Jackson, *A Dictionary of Scripture Proper Names* (Loizeaux Brothers, 1909).

LESSON TWO

TYPES AND SHADOWS, NOT EXACT IMAGES

> ***For the law having a shadow of good things to come, and not the very image of the things,*** *can never with those sacrifices which they offered year by year continually make the comers thereunto perfect* (Hebrews 10:1).
>
> *Let no man therefore judge you in meat, or in drink, or in respect of an holyday, or of the new moon, or of the Sabbath days:* ***Which are a shadow of things to come; but the body is of Christ*** (Colossians 2:16-17).

At best, a shadow of something offers only a silhouette of itself. By turning the object or moving the light, one might obtain a better or different view, but regardless, there is a limited amount of information that one can obtain from a shadow. So it is with the Law.

Nevertheless, the spiritual information that the Law contains is of utmost importance. Although the Law is but a shadowy image of the eternal truth, it is a necessary one. Without the Law, not only would people be unaccountable for sin, we wouldn't even know what sin is! The Law identifies sin—*"sin is the transgression of the Law"*—and it also makes us accountable (1 John 3:4). But at the same time, it also provides for our salvation from sin! Except the Law had said, *"...Cursed is every one that hangs on a tree"* (Gal. 3:13 NKJV), God's spotless Lamb could not have become sin for us. But through the curse of the Law, God *"hath made Him to be sin for us, who knew no sin; that we might be made the righteousness of God in Him"* (2 Cor. 5:21).

Examples of Shadows/Types

Let's take a look at some interesting shadows, or "types," as they are sometimes called.

The first one we'll discuss is when Jacob, with the help of his mother, deceived his father. In my opinion, this is one of the most beautiful passages of Scripture in the entire Bible! You'll see why in a moment.

As you study this type, remember that Paul said the body that cast the shadow is Christ, so we can expect to learn something about Christ in each and every shadow. Some reveal His divine nature, some His supernatural attributes, some His humanity, some His judgments, some His office and work, and some His heart—this example reveals them all.

> *And it came to pass, that when Isaac was old, and his eyes were dim, so that he could not see, he called Esau his eldest son, and said unto him, My son: and he said unto him, Behold, here am I. And he said, Behold now, I am old, I know not the day of my death: Now therefore take, I pray thee, thy weapons, thy quiver and thy bow, and go out to the field, and take me some venison; And make me savory meat, such as I love, and bring it to me, that I may eat; that my soul may bless thee before I die. And Rebekah heard when Isaac spake*

to Esau his son. And Esau went to the field to hunt for venison, and to bring it.

And Rebekah spake unto Jacob her son, saying, Behold, I heard thy father speak unto Esau thy brother, saying, Bring me venison, and make me savory meat, that I may eat, and bless thee before the Lord before my death. Now therefore, my son, obey my voice according to that which I command thee. Go now to the flock, and fetch me from thence two good kids of the goats; and I will make them savory meat for thy father, such as he loves: And thou shalt bring it to thy father, that he may eat, and that he may bless thee before his death. And Jacob said to Rebekah his mother, Behold, Esau my brother is a hairy man, and I am a smooth man: My father peradventure will feel me, and I shall seem to him as a deceiver; and I shall bring a curse upon me, and not a blessing. And his mother said unto him, ***Upon me be thy curse, my son: only obey my voice,*** *and go fetch me them* (Genesis 27:1-13).

In this story, the patriarch Isaac represents the Law. The Law is the Word, and the Word *is* God the Father! (See John 1:1.) But like Isaac, the Law is blind! It could not look to the end of those things that it required (see 2 Cor. 3:13-15). Although it was ordained unto life, it became death unto all humankind (see Rom. 7:10). But Rebekah knew that within Isaac's soul (the spirit of the Law) there was a blessing to be obtained.

Although the Law required the blessing to be given to the first born son (see Deut. 21:15-17), Rebekah loved her second born, Jacob, and coveted the blessing for him. In this shadow, the first born Esau represents the flesh; Jacob symbolizes the Church; and Rebekah and the goats portray Christ Himself!

The goats were sacrificed for the father so that the promised blessing could be obtained. When he was pleased with the offering, he willingly blessed the one who brought it before him. He thought that Jacob, covered by goat skins, was Esau. When Jacob rightly confessed to Rebekah that he was worthy of the curse, she said, *"Upon me be thy curse, my son: only obey my voice."*

This is exactly what Christ says to each and every one of us when we confess our unworthiness. All that He requires of us is that we obey His voice—the Gospel (see Mic. 6:8). When we obey, He willingly covers us with His blood and takes our curse upon Himself, so that we may obtain the blessing of eternal life! Isn't that beautiful?

The second shadow we'll look at is Joseph and his brethren. But this shadow is so long you'll have to read it for yourself, and then we'll discuss it. Take time now and read Genesis chapter 37 and chapters 39 through 45 (skip chapter 38 for now). Since we know that Jesus is the one casting this shadow, we know the interpretation will be about Him.

The first thing we should notice is that Joseph was his father's favorite son, and until Benjamin was born, the only son of his mother—even as Jesus was the Father's beloved Son, and until the Church was born, the only Son of His mother (not Mary, His spiritual mother, which is Jerusalem from above; see Gal. 4:26). So, even from the beginning, we can see that Joseph represents Christ.

Joseph was only 17 years old when he received the promise that his brethren would bow to him. Seventeen means immature,[1] and Jesus was recognized by the Wise Men as King of the Jews even in His infancy. Of course the Jews are Christ's brethren, and although they haven't bowed before Him yet, they will, in time, when God completely fulfills this prophetic shadow.

The second thing to notice is that Joseph's brethren envied him, and because of envy, they threw him into a pit and then sold him into slavery. Then to cover their tracks, they took Joseph's coat and dipped it into blood and gave it to his father. Of course this portion of the shadow portrays the temptations and persecutions of Christ (see Mark 15:9-10).

While in Potiphar's house, although completely innocent, Joseph was accused of an injustice and thrown into prison, just as Christ was unjustly accused and crucified. Joseph's time in prison corresponds to Christ's time in hell (see Rom. 14:9; Acts 2:31). During his term in prison, Joseph pronounced the *temporary* fate of the butler and the baker by interpreting their dreams; but Jesus, while in hell, judged the spirits of the dead with *eternal* judgment (see 1 Pet. 3:18-19; 4:6).

Then comes the resurrection! After Pharaoh had a couple of dreams that he couldn't interpret, the forgetful butler remembered Joseph. When he told Pharaoh of Joseph's expertise in dream interpretation, Pharaoh called Joseph forth from prison. Of course, this portrays Jesus being called forth from the grave. After coming out of prison, Joseph changed his clothes and shaved his beard. This is a type of Christ's glorification. Changing his clothes reflects Christ's resurrected body, and shaving his face is Christ removing the covering of the Law and revealing God's heart through the cross. Joseph's beard is not unlike Moses' veil. Both are symbolic (see 2 Cor. 3:13-16).

Likewise, when Jesus walked among His brethren, they were unable to recognize Him for who He really was. His heart was hidden from them by the veil of His flesh, but since His resurrection, He no longer wears a veil. His heart is open for everyone to see.

After Joseph correctly interpreted Pharaoh's dreams, he was exalted to the king's right hand, as Jesus was exalted to the Father's right hand. There are many more similitudes in these Scriptures:

the king's ring, the fine linen, the gold chain, and so forth, but I will explain only a few more. We need to examine Benjamin, Joseph's younger brother.

Apparently, Benjamin was still an infant when Joseph was sold into slavery, so, at the time of Joseph's release, neither man knew the other by sight (we walk by faith, not by sight). After their first encounter, Benjamin was given Joseph's silver cup, and because he had the cup, he became Joseph's servant forever. Jesus offers us the cup of salvation, and whoever receives it obtains eternal life (silver is symbolic; it depicts *knowledge*).[2]

> *Grace and peace be multiplied unto you through the **knowledge** of God, and of Jesus our Lord, according as His divine power hath given unto us **all things that pertain unto life and godliness, through the knowledge of Him** that hath called us to glory and virtue* (2 Peter 1:2-3).

As Joseph said:

> *God sent* [Jesus] *before you to preserve you a posterity in the earth, and to save your lives by a great deliverance. So now it was not you* [Jewish brethren] *that sent me hither, but God: and He hath made me...lord of all his house, and a ruler throughout all the* [earth] (Genesis 45:7-8).

ASSIGNMENT: LESSON TWO

1. A. In Old Testament shadows, do women sometimes represent Christ?

   B. If so, why?

2. A. In shadows, do you think women may represent a specific role?

   B. If so, what?

3. What is another name sometimes used for Old Testament shadows?
4. A. Who does Benjamin represent?
   B. Explain why.
   C. Why do you think Joseph gave him five times more than his brethren? (See Genesis 43:29-34.)
5. A. What does a beard symbolize?
   B. Although it was socially acceptable for men to wear beards in Joseph's day, he shaved when he was released from prison. Why?
6. Besides those we've discussed, name three more spiritual truths that we can learn from Joseph's life.
7. Reading assignment: Mark chapter 4.

Endnotes

1. Ira Milligan, *Understanding the Dreams You Dream* (Shippensburg, PA: Destiny Image, 2010), 107.
2. *Ibid.*, 99.

LESSON THREE

ALLEGORIES AND PARABLES

All these things spake Jesus unto the multitude in parables; and ***without a parable spake He not unto them****: That it might be fulfilled which was spoken by the prophet, saying, I will open My mouth in parables; I will utter things which have been kept secret from the foundation of the world* (Matthew 13:34-35).

The Synoptic Gospels are filled with parables, and the Law is filled with allegories (see Gal. 4:24). The dictionary[1] says that an *allegory* "is a literary...device in which characters and events stand for abstract ideas, principles, or forces, so that the literal sense has or suggests a parallel, deeper symbolic sense." For example, John Bunyan's *Pilgrim's Progress* is considered an allegory. From this definition one can see that Joseph's life, which we studied in Lesson Two, was a living allegory of Christ's. Likewise, a *parable* is defined as "A simple story illustrating a moral or religious lesson."[2] Thus one can see there is little difference between the two, except possibly an allegory is longer and more detailed than a parable.

Anytime Jesus was speaking before a mixed audience, Matthew tells us that it was always in parables. Because He did not always take the time to say whether He was drawing from actual events, or simply making up a story to illustrate His point, some of His "parables" are debated as to whether they should really be considered as parables or not. But one can see from the definitions given, where the story comes from doesn't define a parable—what the story is illustrating does.

Regardless of whether one is examining living parables or imaginary stories, the method of interpreting them remains the same. Jesus taught us how in one of His many discourses with His disciples. Let's examine one in-depth.[3]

> *Hearken; Behold, there went out a sower to sow: and it came to pass, as he sowed, some fell by the way side, and the fowls of the air came and devoured it up. And some fell on stony ground, where it had not much earth; and immediately it sprang up, because it had no depth of earth: But when the sun was up, it was scorched; and because it had no root, it withered away. And some fell among thorns, and the thorns grew up, and choked it, and it yielded no fruit. And other fell on good ground, and did yield fruit that sprang up and increased; and brought forth, some thirty, and some sixty, and some an hundred. And he said unto them, He that hath ears to hear, let him hear. And when he was alone, they that were about him with the twelve asked of him the parable. And he said unto them, Unto you it is given to know the mystery of the kingdom of God: but unto them that are without, all these things are done in parables: That seeing they may see, and not perceive; and hearing they may hear, and not understand; lest at any time they should be converted, and their sins should be forgiven them.* ***And He said unto them, Know ye not this parable? and how then will ye know all parables?*** (Mark 4:3-13)

This parable is extremely important because Jesus said that the way He interpreted this parable is the way to understand *all* parables! By examining Jesus' interpretation, one can see that He simply replaced each symbol in the parable with its respective meaning. Usually one word, or the thought contained in that word, was sufficient to give them the understanding that He wanted them to have. I have inserted some additional symbolic meanings into His interpretation below to clarify and expand the parable even more.

> *The sower* [preacher] *sows* [preaches] *the word. And these are they by the way side* [path of religious tradition, or willful unrighteousness], *where the word is sown; but when they have heard, Satan* [the fowls] *comes immediately, and takes away the word that was sown in their hearts. And these are they likewise which are sown on stony ground* [hard hearts]; *who, when they have heard the word, immediately receive it with gladness* [the joy of salvation]; *and have no root* [conviction or steadfastness] *in themselves, and so endure but for a time: afterward, when affliction* [trouble] *or persecution* [opposition, rejection, etc.] *arises for the word's sake, immediately they are offended. And these are they which are sown among thorns* [debts, natural responsibilities, etc.]; *such as hear the word, and the cares of this world, and the deceitfulness of riches, and the lusts of other things entering in, choke the word* [hinder its fulfillment or performance], *and it becomes unfruitful.*
>
> *And these are they which are sown on good ground; such as hear the word, and receive it, and bring forth fruit, some thirtyfold, some sixty, and some an hundred* (Mark 4:14-20).

To further expand this parable, consult the dictionary section entitled "Numbers" in my book *Understanding the Dreams You Dream.*[4] When you do this, you will see that 30-fold means conformed (and therefore accepted), 60 means image, and 100 means fullness, or in this case, full measure. Therefore, the last sentence of this passage can be paraphrased in this way:

And these are they which are sown on good ground; such as hear the word, and receive it, and bring forth fruit because they are conformed to His image and likeness. For this reason they are abundantly fruitful.

Compare this paraphrased interpretation to the following Scriptures:

For whom He did foreknow, He also did predestinate ***to be conformed to the image of His Son****, that He might be the firstborn among many brethren* (Romans 8:29).

Till we all come in the unity of the faith, and of the knowledge of the Son of God, unto a perfect man, ***unto the measure of the stature of the fullness of Christ*** (Ephesians 4:13).

If ye abide in Me, and My words abide in you, ye shall ask what ye will, and it shall be done unto you. ***Herein is My Father glorified, that ye bear much fruit;*** *so shall ye be My disciples* (John 15:7-8).

There is one book in the Bible that was written specifically to help us understand parables—the Book of Proverbs.

The proverbs of Solomon the son of David, king of Israel; to know wisdom and instruction; to perceive the words of understanding; to receive the instruction of wisdom, justice, and judgment, and equity; to give subtlety to the simple, to the young man knowledge and discretion. A wise man will hear, and will increase learning; and a man of understanding shall attain unto wise counsels: ***To understand a proverb, and the interpretation;*** *the words of the wise, and their dark sayings* (Proverbs 1:1-6).

Not only do its short, witty statements directly unlock many of the Scripture's mysteries, its method of comparing natural things with spiritual is the epitome of the proper way to interpret parables. For example, putting Proverbs 26:11 and 26:17

together, we have, *"As a dog returns to his vomit, so a fool returns to his folly....He that passes by, and meddles with strife belonging not to him, is like one that takes a dog by the ears."* Here, an offended, biting dog is compared to strife, and the person who incessantly meddles with him to a fool. It doesn't get any clearer than that!

Everyone's familiar with the so-called "dietary laws" of the Old Testament, but few know what they are really for. Jesus' reproof of the Pharisees in Mark 7:14-23 and His disciples' question following it shows that they are actually parables. In fact, Moses' Law contains many parables (see Heb. 8:5; 9:9,23-24; 10:1). There's one law that applies directly to what we are studying:

> *Nevertheless these shall ye not eat of them that chew the cud, or of them that divide the hoof: as the camel, because he cheweth the cud, but divideth not the hoof; he is unclean unto you....And the swine, though he divide the hoof, and be clovenfooted, yet he cheweth not the cud; he is unclean to you* (Leviticus 11:4-7).

The parable in this law is this: If you are to follow God—that is, walk in the Spirit—you must walk in obedience to His Word. You cannot do that without first dividing it. So to illustrate that point, God said if you eat (partake) of His Word without properly dividing it, it becomes unclean to you. Likewise, if you don't "chew the cud," that is, meditate upon His Word day and night so that you can fully obey it, you're unclean (see Josh. 1:8; James 4:17). Only those who will spend the time and effort to meditate upon the Word, dividing the natural from the spiritual, are considered clean in His sight.

It's interesting to note that God requires both. Every disciple is expected to personally meditate, rightly divide, and willingly obey the Word. Christians cannot walk in blind obedience and please God. He wants us to understand His ways and joyfully fulfill His will.

This truth is reflected in several other Scriptures. For instance, have you ever wondered why preachers have beautiful *feet?*

> *And how shall they preach, except they be sent? as it is written,* ***How beautiful are the feet of them that preach the gospel of peace,*** *and bring glad tidings of good things!* (Romans 10:15)

Or this one:

> ***Keep thy foot*** *when thou goest to the house of God, and be more ready to hear, than to give the sacrifice of fools: for they consider not that they do evil. Be not rash with thy mouth, and let not thine heart be hasty to utter any thing before God: for God is in heaven, and thou upon earth: therefore let thy words be few* (Ecclesiastes 5:1-2).

Why Parables?

Why did God choose to use parables instead of simply saying what He meant (see Ps. 78:1-2)? The disciples asked the same question, and the answer may not be as simple as you think:

> *And the disciples came, and said unto Him, Why speakest Thou unto them in parables? He answered...Because it is given unto you to know the mysteries of the kingdom of heaven, but to them it is not given. For whosoever hath, to him shall be given, and he shall have more abundance: but whosoever hath not, from him shall be taken away even that he hath. Therefore speak I to them in parables: because they seeing see not; and hearing they hear not, neither do they understand. And in them is fulfilled the prophecy of Esaias [Isaiah], which saith, By hearing ye shall hear, and shall not understand; and seeing ye shall see, and shall not perceive: For this people's heart is waxed gross, and their ears are dull of hearing, and their eyes they*

> *have closed; lest at any time they should see with their eyes, and hear with their ears, and should understand with their heart, and should be converted, and I should heal them* (Matthew 13:10-15).

With God, it's all or none! He speaks in parables so that we will either, *"know the mysteries of the Kingdom of heaven,"* or we will be completely ignorant of them. Strangely enough, He either wants us to fully understand them so that we will be fully blessed by the treasures they contain, or He wants us completely blind so that He can be merciful in judgment. Reread Matthew 13:10-15, then read the following—Paul's explanation of Israel's blindness:

> *For I would not, brethren, that ye should be ignorant of this mystery, lest ye should be wise in your own conceits; that blindness in part is happened to Israel, until the fulness of the Gentiles be come in....For God hath concluded them all in unbelief, that He might have mercy upon all* (Romans 11:25,32).

God wants His people to hunger and thirst for Him. He's not looking for casual acquaintances. When we sincerely thirst for the personal, experiential knowledge of God, He opens our understanding and freely pours us a big, satisfying drink. When we aren't hungering and thirsting for more and more of Him, He simply leaves us to our own doings and goes in search of someone who *is* hungry.

> *But the hour cometh, and now is, when the true worshipers shall worship the Father in spirit and in truth:* ***for the Father seeketh such to worship Him.*** *God is a Spirit: and they that worship Him must worship Him in spirit and in truth* (John 4:23-24).

Jesus said that every mystery is going to be revealed. How much understanding are you asking for? How much are you willing to receive? How much do you really want?

For nothing [no spiritual mystery] is secret, that shall not be made manifest; neither any thing hid, that shall not be known and come abroad. Take heed therefore how ye hear: for whosoever hath [an ear to hear], to him shall be given; and whosoever hath not, from him shall be taken even that which he seemeth to have (Luke 8:17-18).

ASSIGNMENT: LESSON THREE

1. What is a parable?
2. A. Is Luke 16:19-31 a parable?
   B. How do you know one way or the other?
3. Explain Luke 6:47-49.
4. What book of the Bible was specifically written to help unlock the mysteries hidden in parables?
5. A. What does divided hooves and chewing cuds have to do with walking in the Spirit?
   B. Swine have divided hooves. Why are they still considered unclean under Moses' Law?
6. Why does God speak in parables? Why not just speak plainly?
7. Reading assignment: Proverbs (all).

Now the parable is this: The seed is the word of God (Luke 8:11).

Endnotes

1. *American Heritage Talking Dictionary* (The Learning Company, Inc., 1996).
2. *Ibid.*
3. Ira Milligan, *Understanding the Dreams You Dream* (Shippensburg, PA: Destiny Image, 1997), 27-30.
4. *Ibid.*

LESSON FOUR

UNDERSTANDING SYMBOLS

We've often heard the expression, "A picture is worth a thousand words," and indeed, some pictures are actually easier to understand than words. A good speaker uses illustrations, or *word pictures*, to enable the audience to *see* what he or she is saying. Conversely, parables use *picture words* (symbols), and their meanings must be interpreted. A large portion of Scripture, and most visions and dreams, use symbols to impart their messages. Although a vision may consist of only one symbol, dreams usually contain several. Each symbol, in succession, adds a thought until the message is complete. Learning to understand symbols is similar to learning a new language. In a language, each word contains a specific thought. Likewise, in dreams, visions, and Scripture, each symbol has a specific thought to convey.

Daniel had understanding in all dreams and visions (see Dan. 1:17). Why? Because he understood symbols. Jesus said that we should, too. When Jesus' disciples asked Him why He always addressed the multitudes in parables, He said, *"Because it is given unto you to know the mysteries of the kingdom of heaven..."* (Matt. 13:11). The parables that He taught weren't for the multitudes; they didn't understand them. They were given for the children of the Kingdom! Heaven's mysteries are hidden in the parables of God's Word. If you want to receive the treasures of Heaven, you have to understand symbols. The Word teaches just how to do that.

The Book of Proverbs repeatedly uses natural things (symbols) to reveal spiritual truths. Solomon said he wrote proverbs so that we would *"understand a proverb, and the interpretation; the words of the wise, and their dark sayings"* (Prov. 1:6). By observing how he used symbols, we can learn to understand and use them ourselves. For example, notice how both Solomon and Paul used natural treasures to illustrate spiritual riches in the following Scriptures:

> *My son, if you receive my words, and treasure my commands within you, so that you incline your ear to wisdom, and apply your heart to understanding; yes, if you cry out for discernment, and lift up your voice for understanding, if you seek her as* ***silver****, and search for her as for hidden treasures; then you will understand the fear of the Lord, and find the knowledge of God* (Proverbs 2:1-5 NKJV).

> *That their hearts might be comforted, being knit together in love, and unto all* ***riches*** *of the full assurance of understanding, to the acknowledgment of the mystery of God, and of the Father, and of Christ; in whom are* ***hid*** *all the* ***treasures*** *of wisdom and knowledge* (Colossians 2:2-3).

After reading that, it's not hard to know what Luke 16:11 is all about, is it? *("If therefore ye have not been faithful in the unrighteous mammon, who will commit to your trust the true riches?")* Jesus' comparison of "unrighteous mammon" and "true riches" is the same comparison Solomon makes between silver and the knowledge of God. Paul goes even further, showing that wisdom and knowledge equals understanding, and full understanding is equal to faith—the currency of the Kingdom! There are many things that silver can't buy; but through faith, all things are available! Humankind's wealth, like wine, is but a mocker of that which is *really* valuable (see Prov. 20:1).

Proverbs 11:22 is another good illustration: *"As a jewel of gold in a swine's snout, so is a fair woman which is without discretion."* A hog with gold jewelry in its mouth is compared to a foolish, though beautiful, woman. With that understanding, Jesus' parable, *"Give not that which is holy unto the dogs, neither cast ye your pearls before swine, lest they trample them under their feet, and turn again and rend you"* (Matt. 7:6), makes even more sense, doesn't it? If you try to give spiritual treasures to those who cannot discern their true value (have no discretion), you do so to your own hurt!

Now, what about longer parables? In the same way that multiple words compose complete sentences, multiple symbols reveal complete truths or messages. Pharaoh's dream is a good example.

> *Then it came to pass, at the end of two full years, that Pharaoh had a dream; and behold, he stood by the river. Suddenly there came up out of the river seven cows, fine looking and fat; and they fed in the meadow. Then behold, seven other cows came up after them out of the river, ugly and gaunt, and stood by the other cows on the bank of the river. And the ugly and gaunt cows ate up the seven fine looking and fat cows. So Pharaoh awoke* (Genesis 41:1-4 NKJV).

According to Joseph's interpretation, the seven fat cows meant seven years of prosperity, and the seven gaunt cows meant seven years of famine, which would consume all the previous years' prosperity (see Gen. 41:25-32). How did Joseph know that seven cows meant seven years? Probably because the cows came up out of the river, and a flowing river may speak of time in the same manner that we do when we say, "A lot of water has passed under the bridge since then." Likewise, he knew the cows represented prosperity because cattle were a prime source of food and wealth in his day. (We still use the phrase *bull market* to indicate a rising stock market.)

Although this book is primarily intended to teach you how to rightly divide Scripture, there are times when it's important to be able to correctly discern what God is saying when He chooses to communicate by other means, such as through prophecy or dreams and visions. According to Scripture, He still uses all three.

Peter prophesied that in the last days, *"your daughters shall prophesy, and your young men shall see visions, and your old men shall dream dreams"* (Acts 2:17). When He chooses to speak through dreams, sometimes He uses symbols that are not found in Scripture. In fact, He may use something that wasn't even invented when the Bible was written. Still, there are certain things common to all symbols, and once we understand that, it opens the eyes of our understanding concerning all of them, regardless of their source.

Four Ways

There are four primary ways that symbols acquire specific meanings: One, and probably the most common, is by the symbol's *inherent character*. Because a symbol's basic characteristics are the same the world over, this is sometimes referred to as a symbol's *universal* meaning. For instance, in the Bible, God used innocent lambs to represent His little ones, and merciless wolves to describe their enemies. The descriptive nature, or character of these two animals clearly illustrates what they're depicting (see Luke 10:3; Acts 20:29).

Another way a symbol may obtain a specific meaning is through a dreamer's *personal experience*. An object, animal, person, etc. may mean something to one person that it would not mean to another. A good example is a pet dog or cat. Although dogs are always used in a negative context in Scripture, a personal pet may denote something precious instead of something bad because of the owner's love for it. Another example would be one's childhood home or toys. The one who experienced them would see them differently from how strangers would envision them.

The Bible has an interesting precedent for personal experience influencing spiritual perception:

> *And out of the ground the Lord God formed every beast of the field, and every fowl of the air; and brought them unto Adam to see what he would call them:* ***and whatsoever Adam called every living creature, that was the name thereof*** (Genesis 2:19).

In other words, God speaks our language. Often the way we perceive something carries over into our dreams, even when our perception is less than perfect. Of course this doesn't apply when we're interpreting Scripture.

A third way symbols acquire meaning is through society. Our *culture* may influence our perception of certain symbols and give them special meaning. If someone says that a disgruntled employee "has gone postal," most Americans know exactly what is meant. But say that to an assembly in East Africa, and your interpreter will look at you sideways with a funny look on his face! Likewise, there are several sayings and parables in the Bible that people from Western societies find hard to interpret. Even colloquialisms are occasionally used in Scripture.

If someone is unaware of a certain Jewish saying, the person will get the wrong impression of Jesus from the following Scripture passage:

> *And he [Jesus] said unto another, Follow me. But he said, Lord,* ***suffer me first to go and bury my father.*** *Jesus said unto him, Let the dead bury their dead: but go thou and preach the kingdom of God* (Luke 9:59-60).

Although it sounds like Jesus was being incredibly hard, that's not the case. This man's father was still alive. When the man said, "suffer me first to go bury my father," he actually meant, "Wait until after my father dies and I get my inheritance, then I'll follow you." Jesus was directly addressing this man's covetousness. He challenged him to forsake his inheritance and take up his cross.

If we are trying to help someone interpret a dream and we're unaware of their cultural perception of a symbol used in it, there's no possible way that we can offer them a correct interpretation.

On the other hand, some symbols first acquire meaning in one culture and later become accepted worldwide. A prime example is a red cross. Although it has no inherent character of its own, it has come to mean *first aid* regardless of what nation one is from.

And last, as we've discussed previously, a symbol acquires meaning by the way it is used in *Scripture*. By studying the various ways symbols are used in the Bible, we can see exactly what they mean in our dreams. Sometimes there's no other dependable source of information available. When a dream is from God (and many are), because God does not change, we can always depend upon the *"more sure word of prophecy"* to show us exactly what He means (see 2 Pet. 1:19).[1]

When interpreting symbols used *in* Scripture, it is of utmost importance that we only interpret them *by* Scripture! Peter said, *"...no prophecy of the scripture is of any private interpretation"* (2 Pet. 1:20). If we use our personal or cultural understanding when interpreting the Bible, we *will* end up in error!

ASSIGNMENT: LESSON FOUR

1. Where did Jesus say that God hid the mysteries of the Kingdom?
2. What are the true riches of Luke 16:11?
3. In Pharaoh's dream, how did Joseph know that cows meant prosperity?
4. Does God still speak to us in dreams today?
5. Name four ways that symbols acquire meaning.
6. Which of the four is sometimes known as a symbol's *universal* meaning?
7. Reading assignment: Exodus chapter 32; Daniel chapter 9

Endnote

1. This discourse on the four ways that symbols acquire meaning is adapted from Ira Milligan, *Understanding the Dreams You Dream, Vol. II* (Destiny Image, 2010), 2-4.

LESSON FIVE

EXAMPLES TO LIVE BY

Paul, through the inspiration of the Holy Spirit, called the entire Old Testament, both the Law and the prophets, by one term—*the Law* (see 1 Cor. 14:21,34; Gen. 3:16). When we rightly divide the Law, separating the natural from the spiritual, we realize that the natural commandments and ordinances of the Law produce bondage, while the spirit of the Law brings forth liberty. But many of the natural aspects of the Law are not commandments at all, but rather examples to live by. Also, some are examples of God's severe judgments upon sin.

Paul's converts in Corinth had fallen into error and immorality, and in the following passage of Scripture, Paul admonished them using several examples from Israel's wanderings in the wilderness. He used Israel's disobedient conduct to show the Corinthians God's displeasure with, and the ultimate consequences of, their sin.

> *Now* ***these things were our examples****, to the intent we should not lust after evil things, as they also lusted. Neither be ye idolaters, as were some of them; as it is written, The people sat down to eat and drink, and rose up to play. Neither let*

> *us commit fornication, as some of them committed, and fell in one day three and twenty thousand. Neither let us tempt Christ, as some of them also tempted, and were destroyed of serpents. Neither murmur ye, as some of them also murmured, and were destroyed of the destroyer. Now all these things happened unto them for ensamples: and* ***they are written for our admonition****, upon whom the ends of the world are come* (1 Corinthians 10:6-11).

So in addition to containing the spiritual treasures that are only revealed by the Spirit, the Law openly gives many examples of right and wrong motives, words, and actions to judge our lives by (see 1 Cor. 2:9-10). When David committed adultery with Bathsheba and then had Uriah killed, God reacted swiftly. He sent Nathan to David with a message hidden within a parable. When David judged the man in Nathan's parable, he judged himself (see Matt. 12:37). David pronounced his own sentence of death and retribution.

When He repented, God instantly forgave him, but told him that the sword would never leave his house (see 2 Sam. 12:10-13). Even though God's mercies granted David eternal life, he still reaped what he sowed. This sobering example is recorded to give us the assurance of both God's mercy and His righteous judgments. Even heart-felt repentance doesn't change the eternal law of harvest, "*...Whatsoever a man soweth, that shall he also reap*" (Gal. 6:7; see Gen. 8:22).

Patterns

Although much of the New Testament is divided differently from the Old, it also contains examples of right and wrong conduct (we'll study New Testament division in Lesson Six). These examples are also called "patterns." Both negative and positive examples are found in both Testaments. In the New Testament, Paul said that even his sufferings were a pattern for us to follow:

> *Howbeit for this cause I obtained mercy, that in me first Jesus Christ might shew forth all longsuffering, for a pattern to them which should hereafter believe on Him to life everlasting* (1 Timothy 1:16).

Another type of New Testament pattern is the way God had the apostles conduct their ministries. The early chapters of Acts give many patterns for proper church organization and expansion. Paul's epistles are also filled with instructions and examples.

> *For this cause have I sent unto you Timothy, who is my beloved son, and faithful in the Lord, who shall bring you into* ***remembrance of my ways*** *which be in Christ,* ***as I teach every where in every church*** (1 Corinthians 4:17).

Paul's ways should still be our ways. Our modern methods don't work nearly as well as his old ones did. His turned the world upside down. Ours, far too often, conform to the world rather than transforming the world. Part of our study should be to discover his and the other apostles' ways so that we can achieve similar results.

Paul's sufferings and ways weren't the only patterns that he laid down for us to follow. His integrity in handling finances was impeccable (see 2 Cor. 8:19-21).

> *Therefore watch, and remember, that by the space of three years I ceased not to warn every one night and day with tears....I have coveted no man's silver, or gold, or apparel. Yea, ye yourselves know, that these hands have ministered unto my necessities, and to them that were with me. I have shown you all things, how that so laboring ye ought to support the weak, and to remember the words of the Lord Jesus, how He said, It is more blessed to give than to receive* (Acts 20:31-35).

Of course, the greatest example of all is Jesus. Imitate Him!

For even hereunto were ye called: because Christ also suffered for us, leaving us an example, that ye should follow His steps (1 Peter 2:21).

A good, positive Old Testament example is Daniel. Many Christians don't understand the necessity of fasting and confessing their forefathers' sins to rid themselves of the spiritual bondage inherited through ancestral sins. Daniel's prayer and confession wasn't a carnal commandment that was nailed to the cross—it is a spiritual example to live by! (I've shortened the following passage of Scripture for convenience sake, but you should study the whole passage.)

And I set my face unto the Lord God, to seek by prayer and supplications, with fasting, and sackcloth, and ashes: and I prayed unto the Lord my God, and made my confession, and said, O Lord, the great and dreadful God, keeping the covenant and mercy to them that love Him, and to them that keep His commandments; we have sinned, and have committed iniquity, and have done wickedly, and have rebelled, even by departing from Thy precepts and from Thy judgments: Neither have we hearkened unto Thy servants the prophets....Yea, all Israel have transgressed Thy law, even by departing, that they might not obey Thy voice; therefore the curse is poured upon us...because for our sins, and for the iniquities of our fathers... (Daniel 9:3-19).

Daniel's example of praying in spite of an ordinance passed against it is also one that we should emulate (see Dan. 6:7-10).

A beautiful New Testament example is the spirit with which Paul addressed Philemon when he asked him to forgive his former slave, Onesimus:

Wherefore, though I might be much bold in Christ to enjoin thee that which is convenient, Yet for love's sake I rather beseech thee...for my son Onesimus, whom I have begotten in my bonds: Which in time past was to thee unprofitable, but now profitable to thee and to me: Whom I have sent again: thou therefore receive him, that is, mine own bowels: Whom I would have retained with me, that in thy stead he might have ministered unto me in the bonds of the gospel: But without thy mind would I do nothing; that thy benefit should not be as it were of necessity, but willingly (Philemon 1:8-14).

It's obvious that Paul could have kept Onesimus or even demanded of Philemon to release him. But his gentle plea for Onesimus is an example for us all. Paul truly was as he was supposed to be, a *"servant of all"* (Mark 10:44).

Proper Use of Authority

And last, this brings us to the examples of the proper use of authority. It is obvious from reading the New Testament that the apostles were given great authority to conduct the King's business (see Acts 8:14; 11:22; 15:27; 17:15). We're not lacking in authority ourselves. Paul said that we are ambassadors for Christ (see 2 Cor. 5:20). To avoid the prideful snares that many who have gone before us have fallen into, we *must* pattern our lives after the apostles' godly examples.

The apostles' accountability and submission to one another, and their spirit in dealing with each other, is a model of tact and diplomacy. We'll do well to emulate it. As we have seen, the Scriptures teach that Paul's ways are a pattern for proper leadership. An example was his relationship with Apollos:

*...I [Paul] greatly desired [*Apollos*] to come unto you with the brethren: but his will was not at all to come at this time; But he will come when he shall have convenient time* (1 Corinthians 16:12).

It's obvious that Paul didn't try exercising control over Apollos' ministry. Although Apollos refused his request, Paul didn't accuse him of rebellion. The Scriptures record that Paul was *the* apostle to the Gentiles; nevertheless, he didn't judge another man's (Christ's) servant as a rebel when he didn't submit to his desires (see Rom. 11:13; Gal. 2:7-8).[1]

> *And he said unto them, The kings of the Gentiles exercise lordship over them; and they that exercise authority upon them are called benefactors. But ye shall not be so: but he that is greatest among you, let him be as the younger; and he that is chief, as he that doth serve...but I am among you as he that serves* (Luke 22:25-27).

> *Ye call me Master and Lord: and ye say well; for so I am. If I then, your Lord and Master, have washed your feet; ye also ought to wash one another's feet.* ***For I have given you an example, that ye should do as I have done to you.*** *Verily, verily, I say unto you, The servant is not greater than his lord; neither he that is sent greater than he that sent him. If ye know these things, happy are ye if ye do them* (John 13:13-17).

ASSIGNMENT: LESSON FIVE

1. A. What is the law of harvest?
   B. Is it still in affect?
   C. For how long?
2. Name three examples of the law of harvest operating in David's life. Explain what he reaped as a result of his actions in each of the examples you choose.
3. Is Paul's life a good example of the law of harvest? Explain your answer.

4. A. Under similar circumstances, would Daniel's response to the king's commandment in Daniel 6:7-10 be the right thing to do today? Give Scripture to support your answer.
   B. How do you reconcile your answer with First Peter 2:13-16?
5. As God's ministers, are our lives supposed to be examples also? Give at least two Scriptures to support your answer.
6. A. What is the second division of the Word?
   B. What does it reveal?
7. Reading assignment: 1 Corinthians chapter 11; 2 Corinthians chapters 1–3.

Endnote

1. Adapted from Ira L. Milligan, *Euroclydon* (Servant Ministries, Inc., 1999), 145-146.

LESSON SIX

GREAT PLAINNESS OF SPEECH

But if the ministration of death, written and engraved in stones, was glorious, so that the children of Israel could not steadfastly behold the face of Moses for the glory of his countenance; which glory was to be done away: How shall not the ministration of the spirit be rather glorious? For if the ministration of condemnation be glory, much more doth the ministration of righteousness exceed in glory. For even that which was made glorious had no glory in this respect, by reason of the glory that excelleth. For if that which is done away was glorious, much more that which remains is glorious.

Seeing then that we have such hope, ***we use great plainness of speech:*** *And not as Moses, which put a veil over his face, that the children of Israel could not steadfastly look to the end of that which is abolished: But their minds were blinded: for until this day remains the same veil untaken away in the reading of the old testament;* ***which veil is done away in Christ.*** *But even unto this day, when Moses is read, the veil is upon their heart. Nevertheless when it [Israel] shall turn to the Lord, the veil shall be taken away* (2 Corinthians 3:7-16).

The word *plainness* in this passage means "outspokenness, frankness, bluntness."[1] Moses' words were veiled, but Paul said the *"veil is done away in Christ."* How? In the beginning was the Word, and the Word was made flesh. Jesus was the Word of God. He was born under the Law, and like the Law, His natural flesh was a veil that covered His spirit. When His natural flesh died on the cross, the natural aspects of the Law died. Once His flesh was put off, His heart was no longer covered. His heart is open, and His Spirit is available to all who are willing to receive it.

Since the veil was removed through the cross of Christ, with the exception of the Book of Revelation, *the Word that was given after the cross isn't veiled.* (Revelation is "signified" or written in symbols. See Revelation 1:1.) That means the New Testament epistles aren't parables. In them God reveals His heart openly. Understanding this principle keeps us from making the mistake of spiritualizing the apostles' teachings. So the epistles are plain speech, but the Law and the Gospels are veiled. Nevertheless, the Law made preparation for its own unveiling. Moses said:

> *And it shall be on the day when ye shall pass over Jordan unto the land which the Lord thy God giveth thee, that thou shalt set thee up great stones, and plaster them with plaster....And thou shalt write upon the stones all the words of this law **very plainly*** (Deuteronomy 27:2,8).

This commandment is obviously a parable. The stones represent witnesses, and plaster is what held them together. The Church is composed of *"lively stones"* who are Christ's witnesses (see 1 Pet. 2:5). The Church is both covered and held together through the plaster of God's *agape* love, which is the *"bond of perfection"* (Col. 3:14 NKJV). God wrote the Old Testament on tablets of stone, but He writes the New Testament in His children's hearts. As Paul said in the beginning of his discussion about plainness of speech:

> *Ye are our epistle written in our hearts, known and read of all men: Forasmuch as ye are manifestly declared to be the epistle of Christ ministered by us, written not with ink, but with the Spirit of the living God; not in tables of stone, but in fleshy tables of the heart* (2 Corinthians 3:2-3).

So we can see from this example that Paul's words were the unveiling of an Old Testament parable.

> *But without a parable spake He not unto them: and when they were alone, He expounded all things to His disciples* (Mark 4:34).

In the same way that Jesus expounded all things to His disciples when He was alone with them, when the apostles wrote to their converts, they expounded the mysteries contained in the Law. They *"used great plainness of speech."* When someone attempts to change what the Word says, they are changing the words of life and bringing destruction upon themselves. Don't make that mistake!

> *As also in all his* [Paul's] *epistles, speaking in them of these things; in which are some things hard to be understood, which they that are unlearned and unstable wrest, as they do also the other scriptures, unto their own destruction* (2 Peter 3:16).

Although some teachers claim to find mysteries hidden in the apostles' words, Paul denied that any such thing existed. He said, *"For we write none other things unto you, than what ye read or acknowledge; and I trust ye shall acknowledge even to the end"* (2 Cor. 1:13). There was nothing hidden then, nor is there now. Time doesn't change God's Word.

For example, Paul said that a woman would be saved in childbearing if she and her husband continued in faith, love, and holiness with sobriety (see 1 Tim. 2:14-15). Some teachers erroneously say this passage of Scripture is a parable—that Paul is saying the Church will be saved by bringing forth children (getting sinners saved). In the first place, if it's God's Church, it's already saved. But worse than that, this type of exegesis effectively removes the plain truth contained in Paul's words. Paul isn't talking mysteries here; he's talking about natural women in natural childbirth. Notice the setting:

> *And Adam was not deceived, but the woman being deceived was in the transgression. Notwithstanding she shall be saved in childbearing, if they continue in faith and charity and holiness with sobriety* (1 Timothy 2:14-15).

If he's talking about the Church, why bring Adam into the picture? Paul is plainly talking about the curse of "sorrow" that Genesis 3:16 placed upon women after Adam and Eve sinned. After God cursed the serpent, he turned to Eve:

> *Unto the woman He said,* ***I will greatly multiply thy sorrow*** *and thy conception;* ***in sorrow thou shalt bring forth children;*** *and thy desire shall be to thy husband, and he shall rule over thee* (Genesis 3:16).

Although there *is* a parable hidden in this natural curse, Paul isn't referring to it, but rather he's referring to the natural curse itself. This curse is removed when a couple is walking after the truth of the Gospel. Through Christ, godly women are blessed in childbirth, not cursed with sorrow. (Adam's curse of sorrow was lifted, too. See Genesis 3:17; Psalm 1:1-3; Isaiah 1:19.) So when Paul said, *"Christ hath redeemed us from the curse of the law, being made a curse for us..."* (Gal. 3:13), he also included the Genesis curse!

This doesn't mean, as some teach, that a woman's husband should no longer rule over her. When studying and interpreting a doctrine, it is important to research *all* that God has said about it before finalizing your interpretation. The New Testament clearly says, *"The husband is the head of the wife, even as Christ is the head of the church..."* (Eph. 5:23). The words, *"thy desire shall be to thy husband, and he shall rule over thee,"* aren't part of the curse—but rather the *solution* to the problem which caused the curse in the first place!

> *Wives, submit yourselves unto your own husbands, as unto the Lord. For the husband is the head of the wife, even as Christ is the head of the church: and He is the Savior of the body. Therefore as the church is subject unto Christ, so let the wives be to their own husbands in every thing. Husbands, love your wives, even as Christ also loved the church, and gave Himself for it....So ought men to love their wives as their own bodies. He that loves his wife loves himself. For no man ever yet hated his own flesh; but nourishes and cherishes it, even as the Lord the church: For we are members of His body, of His flesh, and of His bones.*
>
> ***For this cause shall a man leave his father and mother, and shall be joined unto his wife, and they two shall be one flesh. This is a great mystery: but I speak concerning Christ and the church.*** *Nevertheless let every one of you in particular so love his wife even as himself; and the wife see that she reverence her husband* (Ephesians 5:22-33).

When Paul said, *"This is a great mystery,"* in Ephesians 5:32, he didn't mean that the doctrine he was addressing was mysterious and hard to understand; rather, he meant the truth that he was explaining by revelation was beforehand hidden within the Law.

> *How that* ***by revelation He made known unto me the mystery****...which in other ages was not made known unto the sons of men, as it is now revealed unto His holy apostles and prophets by the Spirit* (Ephesians 3:3-5).

The mystery of the Church as the bride of Christ was hidden in the shadows of the Law, but is finally revealed through the *"great plainness of speech"* of Paul's revelatory teachings.

In the case of this doctrine (the husband/wife relationship being a parable of the Church as the Bride of Christ), Paul even reveals what Scripture he received his revelation from—the record of Adam and Eve's creation. In fact, we can discover the origin of many of the New Testament revelations by carefully studying the revelations themselves.

Another Spiritual Division

Now before we go further, I must introduce another important division of the Word. Hebrews 4:12 says:

> *For the word of God is quick, and powerful, and sharper than any two-edged sword, piercing even to the **dividing asunder of soul and spirit,** and of the joints and marrow, and is a discerner of the thoughts and intents of the heart.*

The Word *is* God. It expresses His heart. So even after we divide the natural from the spiritual, there is still another division to be made in the spiritual—the soul (thoughts) from the spirit (intents) of the heart.

It's one thing for God to reveal His thoughts; it's quite another for Him to reveal the hidden purposes motivating those thoughts. In other words, in addition to asking ourselves, "*What* did God actually say?" we should ask, "*Why* did He say it? What was His ultimate purpose? His intent?" The answers to these questions will reveal the second division of the Word—the soul from the spirit. This division applies in both the Old and New Testaments.

Flood and Fire

In the Old Testament, God destroyed the earth with a flood. The flood of Noah was literal, but hidden within the story is several beautiful parables. The simplest of all is this: *The flood represents Moses' Law* (see Isa. 55:10-11). The flood destroyed all flesh, and so did the Law. The flood destroyed the world naturally, the Law destroyed it spiritually. But why did God destroy all flesh? Of course the answer is because of sin.

But even deeper still, notice that both the flood and the Law administered mercy right along with judgment. The obedient were spared, the disobedient perished. Also, both ended with an everlasting covenant.

> *And the rainbow shall be in the cloud; and I will...remember* ***the everlasting covenant*** *between God and every living creature of all flesh that is upon the earth* (Genesis 9:16 NKJV).

> *Now the God of peace, that brought again from the dead our Lord Jesus, that great Shepherd of the sheep, through the blood of* ***the everlasting covenant*** (Hebrews 13:20).

Therefore the flood was literal—it actually destroyed all flesh, except for those who believed God's word concerning the promised destruction and were obedient in preparing for it. But it was also a parable of the Law that was to come. But hidden even deeper within this story is the promise of the everlasting covenant of salvation to be revealed by Christ when He came! So from the very beginning, the redemptive work of Christ is foretold even in God's judgments. Christ's shadow reached all the way to the flood (and beyond!).

Both the Old and the New Testaments reveal another type of destruction coming upon the earth—fire! It's coming as a direct result of the world's refusal to obey the plain truth of the Gospel:

> *And to you who are troubled rest with us, when the Lord Jesus shall be revealed from heaven with His mighty angels,* ***In flaming fire*** *taking vengeance on them that know not God,*

> *and that obey not the gospel of our Lord Jesus Christ: Who shall be punished with everlasting destruction from the presence of the Lord, and from the glory of His power* (2 Thessalonians 1:7-9).

This fire is not symbolic. It is the wrath of God. Yet there is even another truth revealed here—God's ultimate purpose—even His wrath is redemptive! (See Habakkuk 3:2.) Jesus said that if He didn't return early there wouldn't be any flesh left on earth!

> *And except those days should be shortened, there should no flesh be saved: but for the elect's sake those days shall be shortened* (Matthew 24:22).

> *And the nations were angry, and Thy wrath is come, and the time of the dead, that they should be judged, and that Thou shouldest give reward unto Thy servants the prophets, and to the saints, and them that fear Thy name, small and great;* ***and should destroy them which destroy the earth*** (Revelation 11:18).

Everything that God does is out of His goodness, even when He punishes the ungodly!

> *But the heavens and the earth, which are now preserved by the same word, are reserved for fire until the day of judgment and perdition of ungodly men.... Looking for and hastening the coming of the day of God, because of which the heavens will be dissolved, being on fire, and the elements will melt with fervent heat? Nevertheless we, according to His promise, look for new heavens and a new earth, in which righteousness dwells* (2 Peter 3:7,12-13 NKJV).

> *For I know the thoughts that I think toward you, saith the Lord, thoughts of peace, and not of evil, to give you an expected end* (Jeremiah 29:11).

ASSIGNMENT: LESSON SIX

1. Does the curse of women bringing forth children in sorrow still apply today?
2. A. What conditions must a couple meet before they can claim the promise of First Timothy 2:14-15?

   B. Can a woman's husband hinder her from obtaining the promise?
3. A. What did Noah's flood represent?

   B. Was the flood literal or figurative?
4. Was God vengeful or redemptive when He destroyed the earth with the flood?
5. A. Is the fire that Peter said will melt the elements with fervent heat literal, or is Peter speaking figuratively?

   B. How do you know?
6. Why would God burn up the earth?
7. Reading assignment: 1 Corinthians chapter 11; 2 Kings chapter 4.

Endnote

1. James Strong, *Strong's Exhaustive Concordance*, Greek #3954.

LESSON SEVEN

TWO OR THREE WITNESSES

God has given us a simple, yet very important safeguard to use when we are interpreting His Word. Every "truth" is written twice, by at least two different writers. No doctrine is correct that is not confirmed by at least two Scriptures, written by two different people. Paul referred to this principle in one of his epistles.

> *This is the third time I am coming to you.* ***In the mouth of two or three witnesses shall every word be established*** (2 Corinthians 13:1).

If this simple rule had been understood in the first part of the 20th century, during the early days of the Pentecostal revival, some of the "holiness laws" that were taught then would never have been introduced at all. For example, women were told that if they cut their hair they were in rebellion and would go to hell.

For the sake of understanding this principle—that every truth is always established by at least two different writers—let's take a closer look at this unique "holiness" doctrine (see 1 Cor. 11:4-15).[1]

Also, notice that in addition to its more obvious problem—that it only appears to be supported by one Scripture—this law has a double standard. According to this legalistic doctrine, if a woman cuts her hair she is in rebellion. If she just cuts the ends off—*if she cuts it at all*—it is judged as short. When a man's hair is long, he is also considered in sin. If he cuts his hair at all, according to the rule used to bind women, then his hair should be considered short; yet, just cutting off the ends isn't enough. He must cut it above his shoulders or it is judged as long.

If a woman only cuts the ends, her hair is short. If a man only cuts the ends, leaving it below his shoulders, it is long! If cutting off the ends causes a woman's head to be "uncovered," then if a man's hair has been trimmed, isn't his head uncovered even if his hair is down to his belt? The truth is, the Scripture tells us that our conscience quite naturally teaches us when our hair is short or long.

Paul said:

> *Doth not even* ***nature*** *itself teach you, that, if a man have long hair, it is a shame unto him? But if a woman have long hair, it is a glory to her...* (1 Corinthians 11:14-15).

Nature refers to one's conscience. The very nature of our conscience is righteousness:

> *For when the Gentiles, which have not the law, do* ***by nature*** *the things contained in the law, these, having not the law, are a law unto themselves: Which show the work of the law written in their hearts,* ***their conscience also bearing witness,*** *and their thoughts the mean while accusing or else excusing one another* (Romans 2:14-15).

Likewise, feelings of shame come from one's conscience. *"If a man have long hair, it is a* ***shame*** *unto him."* So, unless our hair length makes us feel ashamed, nothing is wrong with it. If our hairstyle doesn't condemn our conscience, it is not a factor in our salvation:

There is therefore now no condemnation to them which are in Christ Jesus, who walk not after the flesh, but after the Spirit (Romans 8:1).

Paul tells us that every Word of God must be established in the mouth of two or more witnesses. The legalistic hair doctrine, *as it is taught*, cannot be correct. The length of a woman's hair is only mentioned by one witness, in one passage of Scripture—in the entire Bible:

If the woman be not covered, let her also be shorn: but if it be a shame for a woman to be shorn or shaven, let her be covered. ...Judge in yourselves: is it comely that a woman pray unto God uncovered?...But if a woman have long hair, it is a glory to her: for her hair is given her for a covering (1 Corinthians 11:6,13,15).

Paul is giving us an understanding of the working of our conscience—not defining hair length. He said, *"Judge in yourselves,"* or, as we would say, "Let your conscience be your judge." (Paul didn't say that women can't cut their hair. He said they should not shave their heads or have their hair shorn [the Greek *keiro* (shorn) means sheared, i.e., cutting it very close, as in shearing sheep] (see 1 Cor. 11:13-14, 28-31; Acts 24:16).

Now the end [goal, or purpose] *of the commandment is charity out of a pure heart, **and of a good conscience,** and of faith unfeigned* (1 Timothy 1:5).

Although you may never be confronted with that specific doctrine, there are other tricks in satan's bag that you *will* face, so understanding this principle of avoiding error while gathering truth is important. In fact, it is so important that God will not even judge the world without first giving it at least two witnesses!

> *At the mouth of two witnesses, or three witnesses, shall he that is worthy of death be put to death; but at the mouth of one witness he shall not be put to death* (Deuteronomy 17:6).

That's the main reason Jesus hasn't returned. We haven't finished our job! *"And this gospel of the kingdom shall be preached in all the world for a witness unto all nations; and then shall the end come"* (Matt. 24:14).

When interpreting the Word, even a small error can be fatal:

> *And Elisha came again to Gilgal: and there was a dearth in the land...and he said unto his servant, Set on the great pot, and seethe pottage for the sons of the prophets. And one went out into the field to gather herbs, and found* ***a wild vine, and gathered thereof wild gourds*** *his lap full, and came and shred them into the pot of pottage: for they knew them not. So they poured out for the men to eat. And it came to pass, as they were eating of the pottage, that they cried out, and said, O thou man of God,* ***there is death in the pot****. And they could not eat thereof. But he said,* ***Then bring meal****. And he cast it into the pot; and he said, Pour out for the people, that they may eat. And there was no harm in the pot* (2 Kings 4:38-41).

The *meal* represents the whole Word of God. If we don't take heed and pay attention to all that God has said about any given subject, we definitely won't have the whole truth. Paul said, *"Prove all things; hold fast that which is good"* (1 Thess. 5:21). The first and the only *sure* way to prove what the Word means is with the Word itself. It takes the whole Word, including every witness, to accomplish this. Jesus said that we would live *"by* ***every*** *word of God"* (Luke 4:4). Of course, we should prove the Word experientially after we have proven it scripturally; that is, it should work in our everyday lives.

Take Every Word Into Account

Every word must be taken into account before a doctrine is complete. If Scripture is misapplied, it will lead to error. Therefore, each word must be taken within the context that the writer placed it in. To use Scripture that was written to instruct us about one subject to modify God's Word on another subject leads to "death in the pot"!

A good example is Paul's statement about the equality of the sexes.

> *There is neither Jew nor Greek, there is neither bond nor free,* ***there is neither male nor female:*** *for ye are all one in Christ Jesus* (Galatians 3:28).

Paul meant just what he said, but for those who are misled, that poses a problem—because that's not *all* that he said. When Paul's statement is placed within its original context, we see that it's not saying what it first appears to say at all:

> *For ye are all the children of God by faith in Christ Jesus. For as many of you as have been baptized into Christ have put on Christ. There is neither Jew nor Greek, there is neither bond nor free, there is neither male nor female: for ye are all one in Christ Jesus. And if ye be Christ's, then are ye Abraham's seed, and heirs according to the promise* (Galatians 3:26-29).

Paul is talking about our personal acceptance in Christ, not our respective governmental position in our family or church. To use this Scripture to justify women in headship violates Paul's instructions in several other Scriptures as well as the instructions of several other biblical witnesses (see Gen. 3:16; Isa. 3:12; 1 Cor. 11:3; 1 Tim. 2:12; 1 Pet. 3:1). As discussed in Lesson Six, women are supposed to be under submission, not in authority. (See Exodus 15:20; Judges 4:4; 2 Kings 22:14-16;

Luke 2:36-38; John 4:7,25-30; Romans 16:1-2; Philippians 4:3; 1 Timothy 2:12.) Wives are to be subject to their own husbands as unto the Lord, and although godly women in ministry are both authorized and needed, in my opinion, women in church government are not.[2] Although the doctrine of equating the sexes may be quite popular with America's feminists, it's not popular with God at all. His design was perfect from the beginning. Nothing has changed as far as He is concerned:

> *Likewise, ye wives, be in subjection to your own husbands.... Whose adorning let it not be that outward adorning of plaiting the hair, and of wearing of gold, or of putting on of apparel; but let it be the hidden man of the heart, in that which is not corruptible, even the ornament of a meek and quiet spirit, which is in the sight of God of great price* [or value] (1 Peter 3:1-4).

God's Word never contradicts itself when it is interpreted correctly. In fact, considering the fact that the Scriptures were written by more than 40 different authors over a period of several thousand years, their agreement is nothing short of phenomenal. Their perfect harmony is a strong confirmation of their divine inspiration (see 2 Pet. 1:21).

Many doctrines have more than the necessary two or three witnesses, but some aren't immediately obvious. Sometimes they are hidden in the shadows. For example, the Book of Joshua confirms many of the truths revealed in the Book of Acts.

Both books chronicle the initial expansion of the Kingdom of God. Joshua expanded the natural kingdom, and Peter and Paul led the invasion to establish Christ's spiritual Kingdom. Israel's natural victories in Canaan foreshadowed the Church's spiritual conquests throughout the ages. The principles of warfare are the same, and Israel's natural, visible weapons symbolize *"the weapons of our warfare* [which] *are not carnal, but mighty through God to the pulling down of strong holds"* (2 Cor. 10:4). Many valuable lessons about spiritual warfare can be learned by studying both the victories and defeats of Israel's armies as they took possession of their promised inheritance.

ASSIGNMENT: LESSON SEVEN

1. How many different, scriptural witnesses (writers) should one have before any specific doctrine is accepted as correct?
2. Does the rule of two or more witnesses also apply to a *rhema?*[3]
3. Why is this rule important?
4. How do we obey Paul's command to "prove all things"?
5. Many people believe that one third of the angels fell along with satan when he fell from Heaven. Are there any Scriptures that support this doctrine?
6. Why do you believe what you believe? Is it because you have proved all things, and you are holding fast to that which is good? (see 1 Thess. 5:21). If not, what should you do?
7. Reading assignment: Matthew chapter 24; Galatians chapter 3; Genesis chapter 3.

Endnotes

1. The following discourse on "hair" is adapted from Ira L. Milligan, *Euroclydon* (Servant Ministries, Inc., 1999), 85-87.
2. See Ephesians 5:22; 1 Timothy 3:1-5. For an in-depth study on this subject, see Ira L. Milligan, *Euroclydon* (Servant Ministries, Inc., 1999), 64-70.
3. *Logos* is usually used in the sense of a thought that *has been* expressed (the Scriptures), as opposed to *rhema,* an utterance, or a thought which *is being* expressed, such as a personal prophecy or dream.

LESSON EIGHT

DISTINCT, EXACT, AND PRECISELY ON TIME

Now the Spirit speaks ***expressly****, that in the latter times some shall depart from the faith, giving heed to seducing spirits, and doctrines of devils* (1 Timothy 4:1).

In this passage, the word *expressly* means "out-spokenly, i.e., distinctly."[1] God's Word is extremely precise. He says what He means, and means what He says. But His Word has several distinct levels of interpretation; so if we aren't careful, we may find ourselves disagreeing with other Christians about certain doctrines even when they are actually right. Sometimes the real error is the disagreement itself. When viewing a passage of Scripture from any specific level of interpretation, a person who interprets it from a different level often appears out of alignment with the "truth" as we see it.

One might say that we need to understand *what* God said, what He *meant* when He said it, and even *why* He said what He said before we even begin to agree or disagree with another's interpretation of any given passage of Scripture.

As we saw previously, the spiritual level of the Word is divisible. The Word itself divides the soul from the spirit, revealing a distinction between even the thoughts and intents of one's heart. Close scrutiny reveals a similar division in the natural aspects of the Word also.

The Flesh and the Mind

Our carnal (natural) self has two separate areas of lust, *"the desires of the* ***flesh*** *and of the* ***mind****"* (Eph. 2:3). Our flesh has a passion for pleasure, and our carnal mind craves prestige and power. For example, David's motive for committing adultery with Bathsheba wasn't the same as his motive for numbering Israel. The first was passion, the second, prestige.

Likewise, the literal fulfillment of the Word (which was made flesh) has these same two divisions. But, there is another division that transcends all other divisions of God's Word, including even His purposes. That division is *time.*

> *To every thing there is a season, and* ***a time to every purpose under the heaven:*** *A time to be born, and a time to die; a time to plant, and a time to pluck up that which is planted; a time to kill, and a time to heal; a time to break down, and a time to build up; a time to weep, and a time to laugh; a time to mourn, and a time to dance; a time to cast away stones, and a time to gather stones together; a time to embrace, and a time to refrain from embracing; a time to get, and a time to lose; a time to keep, and a time to cast away; a time to rend, and a time to sew; a time to keep silence, and a time to speak; a time to love, and a time to hate; a time of war, and a time of peace....* ***He hath made every thing beautiful in His time...*** (Ecclesiastes 3:1-11).

When we apply Scripture in an untimely manner, it *always* leads to error. The Jews made this tragic mistake when they judged Christ's first appearance. They rightly believed that when their Messiah came He would be a man of war. As such, they believed that He would destroy all existing kingdoms and set up one eternal Kingdom to rule over the whole world. What was the scriptural basis for their doctrine? Two of many such Scriptures are Exodus 15:3 and Daniel 2:44.

> *The Lord is a man of war: the Lord is His name* (Exodus 15:3).

> *And in the days of these kings shall the God of heaven set up a kingdom, which shall never be destroyed: and the kingdom shall not be left to other people, but it shall break in pieces and consume all these kingdoms, and it shall stand for ever* (Daniel 2:44).

The only thing wrong with their belief was their timing was a little off. Jesus will eventually do exactly what they expected Him to do, but in *His time*, not theirs. So far their timing has been off by about 2,000 years.

The Tribulation Debate

Some Christians are making a similar error in their interpretation of Scripture today. As everyone's well aware, there's much controversy as to whether the Church will go through the tribulation and be tempted to take the mark of the beast or be raptured out beforehand. Who's right? Many, if not the majority of Christians, believe that Jesus is going to return and take them out of harm's way before the great tribulation begins. What's the scriptural basis for their belief? One Scripture is this:

> *For God hath not appointed us to wrath, but to obtain salvation by our Lord Jesus Christ* (1 Thessalonians 5:9).

Are they correct in their interpretation of *what* God said, what He *meant*, and *why* He said what He said? Let's examine several more Scriptures and see if they agree with a pre-tribulation rapture doctrine. As we do, we will quickly see that the Bible is so clear about this matter that *if we dare to believe Jesus' words, this doctrine is not even debatable.* Jesus' exact words were:

> *Immediately after the tribulation of those days...they shall see the Son of man coming in the clouds of heaven with power and great glory. And He shall send His angels with a great sound of a trumpet, and they shall gather together His elect from the four winds, from one end of heaven to the other* (Matthew 24:29-31).

Jesus' words, *"immediately after the tribulation of those days"* cannot be construed to mean, *just before* (pre-trib) or even, *in the middle of* (mid-trib)—they mean exactly what they say; He isn't coming back until *"after the tribulation"* is over. And He's definitely talking about the great tribulation, because He purposely described, *"the tribulation of those days"* in Matthew 24:21:

> *For then shall be great tribulation, such as was not since the beginning of the world to this time, no, nor ever shall be.*

That's about as great as they get!

It's difficult to understand how a theologian could believe that God is not willing to allow us to go through tribulation when Jesus Himself said that we would! He said, "In the world *ye shall have tribulation: but be of good cheer; I have overcome the world"* (John 16:33).

Likewise, the apostles repeatedly said that we would endure tribulation:

> *Confirming the souls of the disciples, and exhorting them to continue in the faith, and that we must through much tribulation enter into the kingdom of God* (Acts 14:22).

For verily, when we were with you, we told you before that we should suffer tribulation; even as it came to pass, and ye know (1 Thessalonians 3:4).

While we're on the subject of timing, notice that Paul said the rapture would occur, *"In a moment, in the twinkling of an eye,* ***at the last trump:*** *for the trumpet shall sound, and the dead shall be raised incorruptible, and we shall be changed"* (1 Cor. 15:52).

Likewise, Jesus said that God would, *"send His angels with a great sound of a trumpet, and they shall gather together His elect from the four winds"* (Matt. 24:31).

Paul's "last trump" and Jesus' "great trumpet" are announcing the same event. The two trumpets tie these two prophecies together.

Some theologians teach that Jesus' prophecy is talking about gathering the Jews (God's elect) after the tribulation is over. If this were true, how could it be announced by, *"a great sound of a trumpet"?* From where did the trumpet blast come? If the rapture is at the *last* trump, isn't it impossible for one to sound after the rapture is over? It's impossible for God to lie, and He certainly knows what *last* means.

God's Word is precise. His timing is crystal clear—the rapture takes place immediately after the great tribulation is over, and it will be announced by a trumpet blast so loud that it will be heard worldwide. It will be playing "taps," because, *"in the days of the voice of the seventh angel, when he shall begin to sound, the mystery of God should be finished, as He hath declared to His servants the prophets"* (Rev. 10:7).

In spite of all the scriptural evidence to the contrary, some Christians still choose to believe in a pre-tribulation rapture.

They believe that God plans on catching away the Church before the tribulation because of what Jesus said about escaping temptation:

> *And take heed to yourselves, lest at any time your hearts be overcharged with surfeiting, and drunkenness, and cares of this life, and so that day come upon you unawares. For as a snare shall it come on all them that dwell on the face of the whole earth. Watch ye therefore, and pray always,* ***that ye may be accounted worthy to escape all these things that shall come to pass,*** *and to stand before the Son of man* (Luke 21:34-36).

The problem with that understanding is that God and people's definition of *escape* aren't the same. In fact, they aren't even similar. This is clearly evidenced in the following Scripture:

> *There hath no temptation taken you but such as is common to man: but God is faithful, who will not suffer you to be tempted above that ye are able; but will with the temptation also make a way to escape, that ye may be able to bear it* (1 Corinthians 10:13).

God's definition of *escape* means to overcome the power of temptation, not avoid experiencing it. And while we're on the subject of experiencing temptation, notice what John said about the mark of the beast in Revelation 20:

> *And I saw thrones, and they sat upon them...and I saw the souls of them that were beheaded for the witness of Jesus, and for the word of God, and which had not worshiped the beast, neither his image, neither had received his mark upon their foreheads, or in their hands; and they lived and reigned with Christ a thousand years....* ***This is the first resurrection*** (Revelation 20:4-5).

Pretty plain, isn't it? Like the *last* trump, there can't be a resurrection before the *first* resurrection, and the first one (rapture) isn't until *after* the saints have confronted the antichrist and refused to "receive his mark." Or, as John said, *"they overcame him by the blood of the Lamb, and by the word of their testimony; and they loved not their lives unto the death"* (Rev. 12:11).

But what about the Scripture that we started with—where Paul said that we aren't supposed to experience God's wrath? *"For God has not appointed us to wrath, but to obtain salvation by our Lord Jesus Christ"* (1 Thess. 5:9). The answer is quite simple—*we're not!* The great tribulation isn't the wrath of God, *it's the wrath of satan* (see Rev. 12:12).

God's wrath is fire from Heaven, not the mark of the beast. Paul said that God's wrath was going to be poured out as a direct result of the great tribulation. The tribulation that He will recompense upon the unbelievers of this world is a destroying, consuming, purging fire—not some kind of economic control accompanied by war and persecution. Nor will it be at the hands of a demonized madman. Jesus will take care of it personally!

> *And to you who are troubled* [have just been persecuted and endured great tribulation] *rest with us, when the Lord Jesus shall be revealed from heaven with His mighty angels, in flaming fire taking vengeance on them that know not God, and that obey not the gospel of our Lord Jesus Christ: Who shall be punished with everlasting destruction from the presence of the Lord, and from the glory of His power; when He shall come to be glorified in His saints, and to be admired in all them that believe (because our testimony among you was believed) in that day* (2 Thessalonians 1:7-10).

Several things happen simultaneously at that time. At Jesus' return, He will both rapture and reward the saints, and the Jews will recognize and acknowledge Him as their Messiah for the first time (see Luke 13:34-35). Paul said, *"If the casting away of them* [the Jews] *be the reconciling of the world, what shall the receiving of them be, but life from the dead?"* (Rom. 11:15). Life from the dead is the first resurrection!

This doctrinal misunderstanding[2] has a lot of people expecting God to do something that He isn't planning on doing—rapturing the saints out before they prove their love for Him to the antichrist! Don't let wishful thinking or fear keep you from embracing the truth. Jesus isn't coming back just yet—He simply will not break His own Word—and as we mentioned previously, we're not finished with our job yet: *"And this gospel of the kingdom shall be preached in all the world for a witness unto all nations; and then shall the end come"* (Matt. 24:14).

But it won't be long now; both Heaven and hell are awfully busy. We might not know the day or the hour, but we sure know the season (see 1 Chron. 12:32; Matt. 25:13; 1 Thess. 5:1-4).

> *For, behold, darkness shall cover the earth, and gross darkness the people: but the Lord shall arise upon thee, and His glory shall be seen upon thee* (Isaiah 60:2).

We can trust God's Word to mean exactly what it says, but we must be very careful to read what it actually says, and not what we'd like for it to say. Scripture is precise. So precise that Paul built an entire doctrine on the foundation of only one word, and not only on one word, but upon the fact that that word was singular instead of plural. Now, that's precise.

> *Now to Abraham and his Seed were the promises made. He saith not, And to seeds, as of many; but as of one, And to thy Seed, which is Christ* (Galatians 3:16).

God's sword is incredibly sharp. Its preciseness *is* its sharpness. When satan devised his diabolical plot to overthrow Adam by getting him to eat of the tree of knowledge, he knew that Adam would not be easy to deceive. Adam knew exactly *what* God had said about the tree of knowledge, what He *meant* when He said it, and *why* He said what He said. But satan knew that Eve didn't. So his plan was to wrest God's words enough to deceive her. His plan worked and brought about her, and eventually, Adam's destruction. He knew that if he could just dull the sword, he could defeat it (see 2 Pet. 3:16).

> *And the Lord God commanded the man [Adam], saying, Of every tree of the garden thou mayest freely eat: but of the tree of the knowledge of good and evil, thou shalt not eat of it: for in the day that thou eatest thereof thou shalt surely die* (Genesis 2:16-17).

> *Now the serpent was more subtle than any beast of the field which the Lord God had made. And he said unto the woman* [Eve], *Yea, hath God said, Ye shall not eat of every tree of the garden? And the woman said unto the serpent, We may eat of the fruit of the trees of the garden: But of the fruit of the tree which is in the midst of the garden, God hath said,* ***Ye shall not eat of it, neither shall ye touch it, lest ye die. And the serpent said unto the woman, Ye shall not surely die: For God doth know that in the day ye eat thereof, then your eyes shall be opened, and ye shall be as gods, knowing good and evil.*** *And when the woman saw that the tree was good for food, and that it was pleasant to the eyes, and a tree to be desired to make one wise, she took of the fruit thereof, and did eat, and gave also unto her husband with her; and he did eat. And the eyes of them both were opened, and they knew that they were naked; and they sewed fig leaves together, and made themselves aprons* (Genesis 3:1-7).

First, notice that satan got Eve to question *what* God said. In the process, the commandment was changed from *"don't eat"* to, as Paul later said, *"touch not; taste not; handle not; which all perish with the using"* (Col. 2:21-22). Any time we modify God's Word, we annul or dilute its power! *"Every word of God is pure...Add thou not unto His words, lest He reprove thee, and thou be found a liar"* (Prov. 30:5-6).

Next, satan attacked *why* God said what He said, with devastating results. Eve fell for his deception—hook, line, and sinker. Then she played the devil's advocate and enticed Adam to fall with her. Like a joint suicide, each gave in to their passions.

Satan won the first round, but the fight isn't over. Our big brother's coming back one more time. He has fire in His eyes and a sword in His hand, and satan knows that he's in *serious* trouble this time. He won't be able to dull this one! That's where the *"wrath of Satan"* comes from. He's mad, and more than that, he's really scared. He knows—yes, he knows—his time is almost up!

> *Therefore rejoice, ye heavens, and ye that dwell in them. Woe to the inhabiters of the earth and of the sea! for the devil is come down unto you, having great wrath, because he knows that he has but a short time* (Revelation 12:12).

ASSIGNMENT: LESSON EIGHT

1. A. In Lesson Seven, we asked about how many angels fell with satan. If Revelation 12:3-4 is used to support the age-old belief that one third of the angels fell with him, does Revelation 1:1 agree with that interpretation?

   B. Why, or why not?

2. A. What is the real meaning of Revelation 12:3-4?

   B. When will it occur?

3. What three questions should we ask about each Scripture before we finalize our interpretation of it?

4. A. When will the rapture occur?
   B. What are some of the signs that Jesus said we will see before He returns?
   C. Are any of these signs visible now?
5. A. Jesus said that no one will know *"the day nor the hour"* (Matt. 25:13) of His return. Does that mean we can't know anything at all about the timing of His return?
   B. What did Paul say about this doctrine?
6. A. Do you think Jesus could come back right now? At this very moment?
   B. Why, or why not?
7. Reading assignment: Isaiah chapter 28; Hebrews chapter 4; Luke chapter 4.

Endnotes

1. James Strong, *Strong's Exhaustive Concordance,* Greek #4490.
2. The pre-tribulation and mid-tribulation rapture doctrine. I have chosen to emphasize this doctrine only to show the necessity of using God's Word to correctly interpret doctrine and establish God's timing, and the error and danger of believing the teachings of people without proving or disproving them for one's self (see Acts 17:11; 1 Thess. 5:21).

LESSON NINE

LINE UPON LINE, PRECEPT UPON PRECEPT

> *Whom shall He teach knowledge? and whom shall He make to understand doctrine? them that are weaned from the milk, and drawn from the breasts.* ***For precept must be upon precept, precept upon precept; line upon line, line upon line;*** *here a little, and there a little* (Isaiah 28:9-10).

Here the Hebrew word *precept* means "an injunction, or to constitute, enjoin."[1] Before we can understand doctrine, Isaiah said that we must be *weaned* (i.e., mature). Why? Because *receiving truth is a matter of the heart, not a matter of the intellect.* First we hear; afterward, we judge what we hear. Our purpose in judging is to determine whether to accept or reject what we've heard (see Zech. 7:11; Mark 9:31-32). Jesus said that unless we were truly seeking the Father's will, we would unwisely reject what He had to say:

> *I can of Mine own self do nothing: as I hear, I judge: and My judgment is just; because I seek not Mine own will, but the will of the Father which hath sent Me* (John 5:30).

Even scriptural "proof" will not change people's minds if their hearts are not in agreement with God's. Consider this old proverb:

A man persuaded against his will,
Is of the same opinion still!

Receiving truth is a matter of the heart far more than it is of the head. Regardless of what doctrine we're considering, if we have an agenda of our own, our hearts will not be open to the truth, regardless of how logically it is explained.

Before rejecting any viewpoint or opinion which is either new or contrary to the one that we've previously believed and trusted in, it is wise to pray and ask God for more grace (see James 4:4-6). John said, *"A man can receive nothing, except it be given him from heaven"* (John 3:27).

If God doesn't intervene and give us the spirit of wisdom and revelation to receive the truth, we will defend our present position even in the face of direct scriptural opposition. Jesus *was and is* the Truth, but even He couldn't change those who had motives other than the one acceptable motive that God approves, the desire to please Him above all else, even at the expense of one's own life.

For instance in Lesson Eight, the actual timing of the rapture in relation to the coming tribulation was shown. Yet, because of fear, there are many Christians who simply will not accept the truth as it is so plainly revealed in Scripture. We are immature in our faith if we believe that God wouldn't allow us to suffer at the hands of the antichrist when so many who have gone before us have already laid down their lives for the Gospel! Mature faith calmly and confidently testifies, "God's grace is sufficient. Not my will, but Thine be done, Lord."

Besides fear, there is another, more subtle side of immaturity that we are subject to—pride. Proverbs says, *"For the commandment is a lamp; and the law is light; and **reproofs** of instruction are the way of life"* (Prov. 6:23). When we are faced with truth that is different from what we presently believe, we must humble ourselves and admit that we've been wrong before we can receive it. If we stubbornly refuse to admit that we're in error, we automatically reject the truth. This foolishness is a product of immaturity:

> *Foolishness is bound in the heart of a child; but the rod of correction shall drive it far from him* (Proverbs 22:15).

Sometimes it takes the painful rod of God's chastisement to open our ears! Then we comprehend the truth and grow in the knowledge of God. But that's the hard way. There's a much easier way. We should simply humble ourselves, open our hearts, and willingly hear (change). Isaiah specifically tells us how to understand doctrine. He said it's simply a matter of placing line upon line and precept upon precept, and then repeating the process (here a little, and there a little). Whole truth is seldom found in only one place. One way that God hid truth was scattering it throughout the Word. Before we can understand it, we have to gather it together.

Gathering It Together

The best way to learn Isaiah's line upon line procedure is to actually do it. By going through the steps, using Hebrews 4:12 (a Scripture already discussed), we can actually *see* how truth is extracted:

> *For the word of God is quick, and powerful, and sharper than any twoedged sword, piercing even to the dividing asunder of soul and spirit, and of the joints and marrow, and is a discerner of the thoughts and intents of the heart.*

This Scripture compares God's Word to a human skeleton. By placing the lines one above the other and aligning each precept, we can perceive things that we can't see any other way. Before assembling our grid, notice that in this Scripture the joints and marrow of the skeleton are mentioned, but the bones aren't. Likewise, the soul and spirit are named, but not the body.

Then, following the same pattern, the thoughts and intents of the heart are mentioned, but the desires of the flesh and carnal mind are left out. In each case, the bones, flesh, and desires are implied instead of named.

	Flesh		**Heart**
Line 1.	(Bones)	Joints	Marrow
Line 2.	(Body)	Soul	Spirit
Line 3.	(Desires)	Thoughts	Intents

Through Isaiah's instructions, by using natural things that we can readily observe, we can learn spiritual things that we have no other way of knowing. Our first column of precepts under Flesh consists of bones, body, and carnal desires. We know that our bones are ridged and inflexible, so everything in this column will have similar characteristics. This reveals that our carnal nature is fixed and unchangeable. This agrees with Paul's assessment of it—that it will not and cannot conform to God's Law (see Rom. 8:7).

Our second column is also quite instructive. Although the nature of our flesh will never change, we know that our joints are quite flexible. Likewise, it is the soul's *conscious* thoughts that allow us to override the inflexible nature of the flesh and serve God in spite of its desires.

So our flesh's nature is a lot like the Law (which became flesh), while our soul is similar to grace, which gives us flexibility and room to grow up into Christ's nature. Therefore, Paul said, *"to be carnally minded is death; but to be spiritually minded* [have spiritual desires and think spiritual thoughts] *is life and peace"* (Rom. 8:6). From this perspective, it's not hard to understand where ridged, inflexible, legalistic doctrines come from, is it?

This perspective also helps explain Paul's reference to joints in his epistles to both the Ephesians and the Colossians (see Eph. 4:15-16; Col. 2:19). The Church is edified through the fellowship that Christians have with one another (see 1 John 1:6-7). Fellowship develops relationships. Increase in the Body of Christ comes from the nourishment that flows down from the head through the various relationships that we form with each other.

Thus, Church growth and personal ministry are products of Christ working through our souls. The soul is where our conscious will is formed. That's the reason Paul said that *we* have to initiate ministry. He told Timothy not to neglect his gifts, but rather charged him to, *"stir up the gift of God"* that Christ had given Him (see 1 Tim. 4:14; 2 Tim. 1:6). Likewise, Peter exhorted us to do the same thing:

> *As every man hath received the gift, even so minister the same one to another, as good stewards of the manifold grace of God* (1 Peter 4:10).

Although we can do nothing of ourselves, and before our ministry can be effective, it has to be performed by the Holy Spirit working in and through us—nevertheless, our spirit is subject to our soul. We must consciously agree with God's prompting within our spirits before we will yield our members to Him (see Rom. 6:17-19).

Paul said the spirit of a prophet is subject to the prophet. We can and should prophesy by faith, not because God makes us speak. Even praying in unknown tongues is an act of faith, proceeding forth from one's conscious will (see 1 Cor. 14:31-32; Rom. 12:1-2,6; 1 Cor. 14:14). Likewise, a minister with the gifts of healing has to activate his faith to heal; an evangelist must use his or her gift to witness, a teacher to teach, and so forth. We are to consciously labor together with God. Spiritual ministry is performed through our conscious will.

Our third column of precepts begins with the marrow of the bones. Proverbs 17:22 says, *"A merry heart does good like a medicine: but a broken spirit dries the bones."* If our bone marrow dries out, we die. Our bone marrow makes our blood, and *"...the **life** of all flesh is the blood..."* (Lev. 17:14; see James 2:26).

There's another Scripture that we should know about that applies here too, *"A sound heart is the life of the flesh: but envy the rottenness of the bones"* (Prov. 14:30). The flip side of this confirms what James said about our spirits; they desire for people to envy us, *"Do ye think that the scripture saith in vain, The spirit that dwelleth in us lusteth to envy?"* (James 4:5). Envy, whether we are envying others or being the object of their envy, proceeds forth from our spirits. If we envy others, we are exalting them. We may not be conscious of it, but we are worshiping them (that's what *hero worship* is all about).

Conversely, when someone is envying us, we are receiving worship from them, and we've become competitors with God! In our vain imaginations, we've become little gods. That was satan's main selling point when he bartered with Eve for control (see Gen. 3:5). Either way, whether we are envying, or being envied, in the same way that it killed her, it will also destroy us if we yield to it.

Next, besides showing us that envy is a destructive product of our spirits, our third column also teaches us that our true, acceptable will lies within our spirit. God works all things after the counsel of His own will (which is in His Spirit). So, too, should we. We should observe and obey the counsel of our spirits as they align themselves with the will of God the Father. Jesus said that our spirits are both ready and willing to serve Him (see Mark 14:38; Matt. 26:41).

More Precepts to Examine

Isaiah said that we should continue this process (here a little and there a little), so let's examine another line of precepts:

> *For all that is in the world, the* ***lust of the flesh,*** *and the* ***lust of the eyes,*** *and the* ***pride of life,*** *is not of the Father, but is of the world* (1 John 2:16).

We can also throw in Eve's temptation along with it:

> *And when the woman saw that the tree was* ***good*** *for food, and that it was* ***pleasant*** *to the eyes, and a tree to be desired to make one* ***wise****, she took of the fruit thereof, and did eat, and gave also unto her husband with her; and he did eat* (Genesis 3:6).

	Flesh	**Heart**	
Line 1.	(Bones)	Joints	Marrow
Line 2.	(Body)	Soul	Spirit
Line 3.	(Carnal Desires)	Thoughts	Intents
Line 4.	Lust of Flesh	Lust of Eye	Pride of Life
Line 5.	Good (Flesh)	Pleasant (Eye)	Wise (Mind)

This adds six more precepts to compare and considerable more information to use as we search out the Kingdom's eternal mysteries. Comparing these six additional precepts helps separate the soul's carnal desire for power from the hidden pride that lurks within our spirits.

When satan tempted Eve, she bought into his lie and paid dearly for her error. But when he tried the same hard sell on Jesus, he got completely different results. When satan tempted Jesus in the wilderness, he first *commanded* Him to use God's power to satisfy His carnal lust for food. When that didn't work, he *showed* Him all the kingdoms of this world. The reason? He alluded to the lust of the eye, hoping to entice Jesus to covet the same power and authority that he himself had fallen for in the Garden. It didn't work. Then he switched tactics and brought Jesus up to the pinnacle of the temple, *daring* Him to cast Himself down and prove that He was the Son of God. Because Jesus crucified His pride long before He faced the cross, satan's third tactic didn't work either (see Luke 4:1-13).

The same method of comparing Scriptures can also be used to investigate God's time table of future events. Time has a process, as in Genesis 4:3, *"And in process of time it came to pass...."* In the following list, the first column is already firmly established, the second column is being established, and the third column must shortly come to pass (or is in the process of coming to pass).

		1517	**1901**	**20??**
1.	1 Cor. 12:28	Teacher	Prophet	*Apostle*
2.	1 John 5:7	Word	Holy Spirit	*Father*
3.	1 John 5:6,8	Water	Spirit	*Blood*
4.	John 14:6	Way	Truth	*Life*
5.	Luke 3:16	Water	Spirit	*Fire*
6.	Isa. 43:1-2	Water	River	*Fire*
7.	Luke 16:16	Law	Prophets	*Kingdom*
8.	John 1:17	Law	Grace & Truth	*Kingdom*
9.	1 Tim. 1:17	Immortal	Invisible	*Eternal*
10.	Rom. 8:30	Called	Justified	*Glorified*
11.	John 1:18	Declaration	Manifestation	*Demonstration*
12.	1 Cor. 12:5-6	Administration	Manifestation	*Operation*

13.	2 Cor. 8:7	Utterance	Knowledge	*Faith-Love*
14.	Eph. 1:17-20	Knowledge	Understanding	*Power*
15.	John 16:8-11	Sin	Righteousness	*Judgment*
16.	Hos. 6:1-3	1st. Day	2nd. Day	*3rd. Day*
17.	Deut. 17:6	1st. Witness	2nd. Witness	*3rd. Witness*
18.	John 5:33-37	John's Witness	Works Witness	*Father's Wit.*
19.	John 4:34	Milk	Meat	*Finish Works*
20.	1 Cor. 15:3-4	Death	Burial	*Resurrection*
21.	John 2:11	Wine		
	John 4:48-54		Signs & Wonders	
	John 12:18		*Raise Dead*	

Looks like some exciting times ahead, doesn't it?

ASSIGNMENT: LESSON NINE

1. A. What, more than anything else, blocks our understanding of "new" truth?
   B. Does this hindrance come from our souls or from our spirits?
   C. How do you know?
2. A. Which wills are acceptable with God, our flesh's will, our soul's, or our spirit's?
   B. Give at least one Scripture to prove that your answer is correct.
3. What other Scriptures can you think of that could be added to the Hebrews 4:12 grid that we studied?
4. A. Is covetousness a matter of fleshly lust or lust that proceeds forth from one's soul?
   B. Is covetousness ever acceptable with God?
5. A. Why is it natural for people to desire others to envy them?
   B. Is this acceptable with God?

6. A. Great athletes and movie stars have fans. Is it all right to be one of those fans, or is it wrong?

   B. Why?

7. Reading assignment: Hebrews chapter 6; Exodus chapter 12; Leviticus chapter 23; Deuteronomy chapter 16.

Endnote

1. James Strong, *Strong's Exhaustive Concordance,* #6673, 6680.

LESSON TEN

FOR MATURE CHRISTIANS ONLY

Important Notice! The following discourse is for mature readers only. Spiritually immature Christians may be offended by the plain truth that is revealed within the following pages.

> *Of whom we have many things to say, and hard to be uttered, seeing ye are dull of hearing. For when for the time ye ought to be teachers, ye have need that one teach you again which be the first principles of the oracles of God; and are become such as have need of milk, and not of strong meat. For every one that uses milk is unskillful in the word of righteousness: for he is a babe. But strong meat belongs to them that are of full age, even those who by reason of use have their senses exercised to discern both good and evil* (Hebrews 5:11-14).

In the previous nine lessons, we covered several important points to consider and use as we rightly divide the Word of God. First we separate the chaff from the wheat, dividing the natural things from the spiritual things contained within the Law, the prophets, and the Gospels. Some are carnal ordinances; others are spiritual principles to live by.

As we carefully observe the natural, historical examples, we also look for the shadowy, hidden mysteries concealed within those same Scriptures. By observing what each different witness contributes and being careful to keep each Scripture within its own context, we avoid error while increasing our knowledge of God. Allegories, parables, and symbols all give us precise timing and instructions in understanding God's will and ways through His Word.

By testing and comparing each revelation and understanding against the revealed truth of the apostles' writings, we prove all things, rejecting error while holding fast to that which is good.

And last, by placing line upon line and precept upon precept, we separate and analyze each precept for complete understanding of *what* God said, exactly what He *meant*, and *why* He said what He said.

Seven Feasts and Precepts

When Moses led Israel out of Egypt, God used the occasion to institute seven feasts that would forever shape the Jewish nation (and their spiritual fulfillment eventually affects the history of the whole world). These seven feasts were as foundational to the Jewish religion as the Gospel is to Christianity.

The feasts were divided into three successive events (see Deut. 16:16; Lev. 23:1-44). The first contained the feasts of Passover and unleavened bread. The second period included the feast of firstfruits and the feast of Pentecost. And the third consisted of the blowing of trumpets, the day of atonement, and the feast of tabernacles.

Passover	Unleavened B.	Firstfruits	Pentecost	Trumpets	Atonement	Tabernacles

As we continue, we will examine the significance of each feast separately, using Isaiah's, *"precept upon precept and line upon line"* method of rightly dividing the Word. But first we will locate another foundational Scripture that contains seven precepts to which we can compare the feasts. There are several, but by using one found in the *"great plainness of speech"* Scriptures, we won't have to divide the natural from the spiritual because the apostles have already done that for us (see 2 Cor. 3:12). Therefore, we can use it just as it is written. Such a Scripture is found in Hebrews chapter 6.

> *Therefore leaving the principles of the doctrine of Christ, let us go on unto* ***perfection****; not laying again the foundation of* ***repentance*** *from dead works, and of* ***faith*** *toward God, of the doctrine of* ***baptisms****, and of laying on of* ***hands****, and of* ***resurrection*** *of the dead, and of eternal* ***judgment*** (Hebrews 6:1-2).

This Scripture contains seven foundational precepts. I've bolded certain key words to identify each precept. As we continue, we will see that although six of these precepts are listed in their proper order, the seventh, *perfection*, is listed at the beginning. This is as it should be, because it gives us our destination—our Christian journey is to seek perfection in Christ. If we don't know where we're going, we're not very likely to get there.

This Scripture fully expands the basic precepts of the Gospel—the death (repentance), burial (baptism), resurrection (eternal life), and witness of the resurrection (appearing) of Christ (see 1 Cor. 15:1-8). Its seven precepts fit the feasts perfectly.

Precept One

The first precept is the key to matching these two lines. The feasts start with the death of *a* Passover lamb and Israel's departure from Egypt, and the Gospel starts with the death of *the* Passover Lamb and a sinner's departure from sin.

Passover	Unleavened B.	Firstfruits	Pentecost	Trumpets	Atonement	Tabernacles
Repentance	Faith	Baptisms	Hands	Resurrection	Judgment	Perfection

This arrangement quickly brings to light some things that are not readily seen when these Scriptures are examined separately. Since the feasts are parables, and the seven foundational doctrines are revealed truth, by comparing one with the other, the doctrines will unlock the parables, and the parables will give additional understanding about the doctrines—some more, some less.

For instance, there's an obvious connection between Passover and repentance—both refer to death. Passover refers to the death of the first born of Egypt and the sacrificial Lamb of God, and repentance refers to dying to one's own self-will. But what, you might ask, does the feast of unleavened bread have in common with faith toward God? The answer is much, in every way!

> *For if our heart condemns us, God is greater than our heart, and knows all things. Beloved,* ***if our heart condemns us not, then have we confidence toward God.*** *And whatsoever we ask, we receive of Him, because we keep His commandments, and do those things that are pleasing in His sight* (1 John 3:20-22).

It is impossible to have faith with leaven in your house (heart). Notice the way Paul dealt with leaven:

> *Purge out therefore the old leaven, that ye may be a new lump, as ye are unleavened. For even Christ our Passover is sacrificed for us: Therefore let us keep the feast, not with old leaven, neither with the leaven of malice and wickedness; but with the unleavened bread of sincerity and truth* (1 Corinthians 5:7-8).

Our hearts are purified by faith. A heart cannot be defiled with sin and be pure at the same time. Faith will not coexist with guilt and condemnation.

Precept Two

Our third column compares the feast of firstfruits and the doctrine of baptisms:

Passover	Unleavened B.	Firstfruits	Pentecost	Trumpets	Atonement	Tabernacles
Repentance	Faith	Baptisms	Hands	Resurrection	Judgment	Perfection

Although this doctrine is too long to adequately deal with here,[1] it's important to know that it's not until we are baptized in water that we are wholly separated from this world and become the firstfruits of God's harvest.[2] James said, *"Of His own will begat He us with the word of truth, that we should be a kind of firstfruits of His creatures"* (James 1:18). And Jesus said, *"Verily, verily, I say unto thee, Except a man be born again, he cannot see the kingdom of God....Except a man be born of water and of the Spirit, he cannot enter into the kingdom of God"* (John 3:3-5).

It's one thing to *see* the Kingdom, but it's entirely another thing to *enter into* it. Sadly, the modern Church has relegated this divine ordinance to a much lower priority than both Christ and the early Church gave it (see Matt. 3:13-16; Mark 16:16; Acts 2:38,41; 8:12; 16:15,33; 19:1-6). Water baptism is the first step to take after a person has seen the Kingdom through the eyes of faith:

> *Then Philip opened his mouth, and began at the same scripture, and preached unto him Jesus. And as they went on their way, they came unto a certain water: and the eunuch said, See, here is water; what doth hinder me to be baptized? And Philip said, If thou believest with all thine heart, thou mayest. And he answered and said, I believe that Jesus Christ is the Son of God* (Acts 8:35-37).

Precept Three

And what about the Feast of Pentecost and the laying on of hands doctrine?

Passover	Unleavened B.	Firstfruits	Pentecost	Trumpets	Atonement	Tabernacles
Repentance	Faith	Baptisms	Hands	Resurrection	Judgment	Perfection

Again, it's a long story, but to keep it short, let's go right to the spiritual fulfillment of what the natural feast promised—the unlimited outpouring of the Holy Spirit. First the fulfillment:

> *And* ***when the day of Pentecost was fully come****, they were all with one accord in one place. And suddenly there came a sound from heaven as of a rushing mighty wind, and it filled all the house where they were sitting. And there appeared unto them cloven tongues like as of fire, and it sat upon each of them. And* ***they were all filled with the Holy Ghost,*** *and began to speak with other tongues, as the Spirit gave them utterance* (Acts 2:1-4).

And then Peter's interpretation of their glorious experience:

> *But Peter, standing up with the eleven, lifted up his voice, and said unto them, Ye men of Judea, and all ye that dwell at Jerusalem, be this known unto you...this is that which was spoken by the prophet Joel; And it shall come to pass in the last days, saith God,* ***I will pour out of My Spirit upon all flesh:*** *and your sons and your daughters shall prophesy, and your young men shall see visions, and your old men shall dream dreams:* ***And on My servants and on My handmaidens I will pour out in those days of My Spirit;*** *and they shall prophesy* (Acts 2:14-18).

Every time we keep the feasts, the same thing happens all over again. The feasts are perpetual. After announcing each feast, Moses said, *"It shall be a statute for ever throughout your generations in all your dwellings"* (Lev. 23:14). The natural feasts were for the natural Jews; the spiritual fulfillment is for every generation of believers. Once God gives us something, He won't take it back. Moses said,

"The secret things belong unto the Lord our God: but those things which are revealed belong unto us and to our children for ever..." (Deut. 29:29). God's gifts are forever! (See Acts 2:38; Romans 11:29.)

One more thing before we pass on to the fifth column. Our second precept (in the fourth column) reveals that the baptism of the Spirit is both received and administered through the hearing of faith and by the laying on of hands (see Gal. 3:2,5):

> *Then [Peter and John] laid they their hands on them, and they received the Holy Ghost* (Acts 8:17).
>
> *And when Paul had laid his hands upon them, the Holy Ghost came on them; and they spake with tongues, and prophesied* (Acts 19:6).

Precepts Four and Five

The next two precepts are the feasts of the blowing of trumpets and the resurrection of the dead.

Passover	Unleavened B.	Firstfruits	Pentecost	Trumpets	Atonement	Tabernacles
Repentance	Faith	Baptisms	Hands	Resurrection	Judgment	Perfection

Most people think that when the writer of Hebrews lists the resurrection of the dead that he's referring to the rapture—and that's what Martha thought that Jesus meant—but the writer isn't, and Jesus wasn't:

> *Then said Martha unto Jesus, Lord, if Thou hadst been here, my brother had not died. But I know, that even now, whatsoever Thou wilt ask of God, God will give it Thee.* ***Jesus saith unto her, Thy brother shall rise again. Martha saith unto Him, I know that he shall rise again in the resurrection at the last day. Jesus said unto her, I am the resurrection,*** *and the life: he that believeth in Me, though he were dead, yet shall he live....Jesus said, Take ye away the stone. Martha, the*

sister of him that was dead, saith unto Him, Lord, by this time he stinks: for he hath been dead four days. Jesus saith unto her, Said I not unto thee, that, if thou wouldest believe, thou shouldest see the glory of God? (John 11:21-25, 39-40)

We need a revelation of God's power for our generation. God wants us to have faith in His power *now*—not at some future date! Paul said that our faith was supposed to stand in the power of God, not in the wisdom of people (see 1 Cor. 2:4-5). He prayed for just such a revelation to be given to the Ephesians (see Eph. 1:16-20). But what does blowing trumpets have to do with resurrection power? The answer is simple; the trumpet's blast is the sound of our voice, and anointed words release divine power:

Cry aloud, spare not, ***lift up thy voice like a trumpet,*** *and shew My people their transgression, and the house of Jacob their sins* (Isaiah 58:1).

God's power is released through the proclamation of His Word. He upholds all things by *"the word of His power"* (Heb. 1:3). When His preachers become courageous enough to boldly and uncompromisingly preach His Word, the power of His Word will raise those who are dead in trespasses and sins, loose those who are bound in the grave clothes of religious tradition, and give life to many with unseeing eyes and deaf ears. Plus, maybe He'll also raise up some of today's Dorcases and Eutychuses who happen to die in the line of duty (see Eph. 2:1; Rev. 3:1; Luke 4:18; Acts 9:36-41; 20:9-10).

Timid preaching and witnessing simply won't get the job done. We have to be empowered by God's Spirit to release His power. Even Paul asked the saints to pray for him to have more boldness. Maybe that's what we should be praying for:

Praying always with all prayer and supplication in the Spirit, and watching thereunto with all perseverance and supplication for all saints; and for me, that utterance may be given unto me, that I may open my mouth boldly, to make known the mystery of the gospel, For which I am an ambassador in bonds: that therein I may speak boldly, as I ought to speak (Ephesians 6:18-20).

And when they had prayed, the place was shaken where they were assembled together; and ***they were all filled with the Holy Ghost, and they spake the word of God with boldness*** (Acts 4:31).

Precept Six

Once God's power is restored to the Church, the same power that raises the dead will "kill the living" (see Acts 5:1-11). That's what the day of atonement and the doctrine of eternal judgment portray:

Passover	Unleavened B.	Firstfruits	Pentecost	Trumpets	Atonement	Tabernacles
Repentance	Faith	Baptisms	Hands	Resurrection	Judgment	Perfection

Peter said, *"For the time is come that judgment* ***must*** *begin at the house of God: and if it first begin at us, what shall the end be of them that obey not the gospel of God?"* (1 Peter 4:17).

Precept Seven

God hates hypocrisy. Before He can judge the world, He must first judge His own house (see Exod. 4:21-26). But that's not long in coming, because He's not long in coming. But before He does, we have to get out into the fields, bring in the harvest, and at the same time get ready for a wedding! That's what the last column, the feasts of tabernacles and the doctrine of perfection, is all about:

Passover	Unleavened B.	Firstfruits	Pentecost	Trumpets	Atonement	Tabernacles
Repentance	Faith	Baptisms	Hands	Resurrection	Judgment	Perfection

Be patient therefore, brethren, unto the coming of the Lord. ***Behold, the husbandman waits for the precious fruit of the earth,*** *and hath long patience for it, until he receive the early and latter rain. Be ye also patient...for the coming of the Lord draws nigh* (James 5:7-8).

Let us be glad and rejoice, and give honor to him: for ***the marriage of the Lamb is come, and his wife hath made herself ready*** (Revelation 19:7).

Are you ready?

The seven precepts and the feasts that we have studied open up many doors for additional study into the depth of God's Word. They also provide a timeline by which Christians can evaluate their personal and corporate progress.

The Next Steps

If a person has repented and through faith in God has been baptized into His name, then the next step is to seek God for the baptism of the Holy Spirit. This may easily be accomplished by having a qualified believer lay hands upon him or her. Once the person has received the Holy Spirit baptism, the next step is to pray for boldness to witness and preach the whole Word of God without compromise. God's power will do the rest!

We need not pray for judgment. His power will also bring us into unity and spiritual maturity (perfection), which is His stated goal. These are impossible for people to achieve through their own efforts (see Eph. 4:3,11-13).

Only God can change a person's heart, and as we've said, accepting truth is a matter of the heart, not the head. God said He's sending strong delusion unto those who aren't devoted to the truth. Those who love truth aren't easily swayed by satan's deceptions. Notice the medium that the antichrist will use to spread his delusion throughout the world—cold hearts void of love for God's truth.

> *And with all deceivableness of unrighteousness in them that perish;* ***because they received not the love of the truth,*** *that they might be saved. And* ***for this cause God shall send them strong delusion, that they should believe a lie:*** *That they all might be damned who believed not the truth, but had pleasure in unrighteousness* (2 Thessalonians 2:10-12).

The most precious treasure Heaven has to offer is *truth!* Jesus promised those who love the truth, *"Ye shall know the truth, and the truth shall make you free"* (John 8:32). As we obey God and make evangelism, spiritual unity, and love for the brethren our foremost priorities, He will perform what He promised and bring the Church into greater unity of the faith. In the process, He will also bring us into spiritual maturity. Then we will all conform to *the* truth, whose name is Jesus.

> ***Endeavoring to keep the unity of the Spirit in the bond of peace.*** *And He gave some, apostles; and some, prophets; and some, evangelists; and some, pastors and teachers; for the perfecting of the saints, for the work of the ministry, for the edifying of the body of Christ:* ***Till we all come in the unity of the faith,*** *and of the knowledge of the Son of God, unto a perfect* [mature] *man, unto the measure of the stature of the fulness of Christ* (Ephesians 4:3,11-13).

ASSIGNMENT: LESSON TEN

1. From memory, list five or more important things you should consider as you divide the Word of God.

2. A. How many times a year were the Jews supposed to gather together before the Lord?
   B. What were they gathering for?
3. A. What is the significance of the feast of unleavened bread?
   B. Why did it last seven days?
4. A. How many days from the feast of firstfruits were the Israelites supposed to count before starting the next feast?
   B. What was the next one called?
5. A. Is there another line of seven precepts that we could put with the two we used?
   B. What Scripture is it?
   C. Would it give us additional information if we did?
6. A. Are we still supposed to keep the Jewish feasts?
   B. Why, or why not?
7. Reading assignment: Deuteronomy 21:22-23; Acts 19:1-7.

Endnotes

1. We will discuss water baptism in Lesson Eleven.
2. I'm not saying that one isn't saved without water baptism, but baptism is the ordinance that removes us bodily from the Law's ordinances (see Rom. 6:6,14; Col. 2:11-14; 1 Cor. 10:1-2).

LESSON ELEVEN

NO OTHER FOUNDATION

According to the grace of God which is given unto me, as a wise masterbuilder, I have laid the foundation, and another builds thereon. But let every man take heed how he builds thereupon. ***For other foundation can no man lay than that is laid, which is Jesus Christ*** (1 Corinthians 3:10-11).

Before building, there's nothing more important than laying a firm, solid foundation. The seven feasts and foundational doctrines discussed in Lesson Ten are the basic principles of the doctrine of Christ. Jesus Christ *is* the Foundation. There is no other. Therefore, to gain additional understanding of the doctrine of Christ, we'll apply Isaiah's method of scriptural interpretation and add another line of precepts to those we've just studied. This time, we'll get them from different places—as Isaiah said, *"here a little, and there a little."*

Although all seven doctrines can be expanded in this way, we will make a detailed examination of only one of them—the doctrine of baptisms.

Therefore leaving the principles of the doctrine of Christ, let us go on unto perfection; not laying again the foundation of

> *repentance from dead works, and of faith toward God, of the* ***doctrine of baptisms,*** *and of laying on of hands, and of resurrection of the dead, and of eternal judgment* (Hebrews 6:1-2).

Doctrine One

Notice the Scripture says *doctrine* singular, but *baptisms* plural. Each of the seven doctrines has a corresponding baptism.

Passover	Unleavened B.	Firstfruits	Pentecost	Trumpets	Atonement	Tabernacles
Repentance	Faith	Baptisms	Hands	Resurrection	Judgment	Perfection
John's B.	G. Conscience	Water B.	Holy Spirit	Power (Fire)	Purification	Suffering

The importance of understanding baptisms is revealed by a revelation that Peter had concerning Noah's flood. Peter realized that we're *saved* by baptism!

> *The like figure whereunto even* ***baptism doth also now save us*** *(not the putting away of the filth of the flesh,* ***but the answer of a good conscience toward*** *God,) by the resurrection of Jesus Christ* (1 Peter 3:21).

Peter is actually discussing two different baptisms here—the baptism of *repentance* and the baptism of *faith.* The one that *saves* us is the baptism of faith. At the time of Noah's flood, the world's baptism *("putting away of the filth of the flesh")* destroyed it, but Noah found grace in the eyes of the Lord. Although he experienced the flood right along with the rest of the world, his faith saved him. He had another baptism the world didn't have. They were buried by the flood in their sin, but Noah was lifted up by *"the answer of a good conscience toward God."* His conscience was clear; his heart was purified by faith (see Acts 15:9). Baptism is a burial, or covering. Noah was supernaturally covered by Christ's blood through faith.

Peter's reference to *"putting away of the filth of the flesh"* is talking about the baptism of repentance, which was preached and administered by John the Baptist. John warned the Pharisees that repentance was a prerequisite for all other baptisms (see Matt. 3:11; Acts 19:4).

> *But when he [John] saw many of the Pharisees and Sadducees come to his baptism, he said unto them, O generation of vipers, who hath warned you to flee from the wrath to come? **Bring forth therefore fruits meet for repentance*** (Matthew 3:7-8).

When a sinner observes the spiritual feast of Passover (repents), his heart is cleansed by the blood so that he can believe God for salvation. Christ is the spotless Lamb that God provided for the Passover sacrifice. After a sinner repents, if he truly believes that God has forgiven him, then *"the blood of Christ, who through the eternal Spirit offered Himself without spot to God,* [will] *purge your conscience from dead works to serve the living God"* (Heb. 9:14). A new believer is saved by grace through faith. It is a gift of God (see Eph. 2:8).

Doctrine Two

This brings us to the second column:

Passover	Unleavened Bread
Repentance	Faith
John's Baptism	Good Conscience

Once we have partaken of Passover, we are to keep the feast of Unleavened Bread. In the same way that Jesus is our Passover Lamb, He is also our Unleavened Bread:

> *This is the bread which comes down from heaven, that a man may eat thereof, and not die. I am the living bread which came down from heaven: if any man eat of this bread, he shall live for ever: and the bread that I will give is My flesh, which I will give for the life of the world* (John 6:50-51).

Jesus is the Word of God. We fulfill the feast of unleavened bread by "eating Christ's flesh"—that is, by reading, meditating upon, and doing the Word of God, which *"is that good and acceptable, and perfect, will of God"* (John 6:53; 4:34).

> *And be not conformed to this world: but be ye transformed by the renewing of your mind, that ye may prove what is that good, and acceptable, and perfect, will of God* (Romans 12:2).

One cannot stay in Egypt and keep the feasts. Although the feast of Passover is kept in Egypt (Christ saves us where we are, and then brings us to where we should be), we are to eat it with our shoes on our feet, ready to go (see Exod. 12:11). The feast of Unleavened Bread is kept in the wilderness. There in the "like figure" of Noah we are separated from this world. Noah rejected *"the world that then was"* (2 Pet. 3:6), believed God, and separated himself by entering the ark.

Doctrine Three

This brings us to our third column, the feast of firstfruits and the doctrine of baptisms (which includes water baptism):

Passover	Unleavened Bread	Firstfruits
Repentance	Faith	Baptisms
John's Baptism	Good Conscience	Water B.

When Noah entered the ark, he became the firstfruits of the regenerated and renewed earth (see Titus 3:5).[1] He was separated unto God and protected from the curse that was poured out upon the world. In like manner, our obedience to the Gospel removes us from under the Law and gives us salvation from this world's curse. Water baptism is part of the Gospel. The Gospel is the death, burial, resurrection, and the witness of the resurrection of Jesus Christ:

> *Moreover, brethren,* ***I declare unto you the gospel*** *which I preached unto you, which also ye have received, and wherein*

ye stand; ***By which also ye are saved,*** *if ye keep in memory what I preached unto you, unless ye have believed in vain. For I delivered unto you first of all that which I also received, how that* ***Christ died for our sins*** *according to the scriptures; and that* ***He was buried****, and that* ***He rose again the third day*** *according to the scriptures: And that* ***He was seen*** *of Cephas, then of the twelve: After that, He was seen of above five hundred brethren at once; of whom the greater part remain unto this present, but some are fallen asleep. After that, He was seen of James; then of all the apostles. And last of all He was seen of me [Paul] also, as of one born out of due time* (1 Corinthians 15:1-8).

We are supposed to follow Jesus' steps (see 1 Pet. 2:21). He gave us an example to live by. When John asked Him why He wanted to be baptized, Jesus replied, *"It becometh us to fulfil all righteousness"* (Matt. 3:15).

As previously mentioned, the Law made provision for our salvation. In the Old Testament when someone accursed of God died, the Law commanded immediate burial: *"Thou shalt in any wise bury him that day"* (Deut. 21:23). Once we've repented (died), we must be buried in obedience to the Law. After we obey the Law, we can rise from our watery grave and walk in newness of life.

The Law has no jurisdiction over anyone raised from the dead. It makes no commandment nor pronounces any curse upon those who have come forth from the grave. Paul said that once we've been baptized into Christ's death, we are free from the Law (see Rom. 6:3-22). Thus water baptism is a divinely appointed ordinance that provides bodily separation from under Moses' Law. It is our final step of obedience in fulfilling the righteousness of the Law.

Our *soul* is separated from the world unto God through the baptism of repentance. Our *spirit* is separated by the baptism of faith, which is the answer of a good conscience toward God. Our *body* is separated through water baptism. Like the thief on the cross, those who believe, yet fail to receive water baptism, ultimately fulfill the Law through natural burial (see Luke 23:39-43). But why wait for death to remove yourself from the many curses of the Law? (See Romans 6:6.) Obey *all* of the Gospel.

The Law said, *"the soul that sins, it shall die"* (Ezek. 18:20). To be saved, we must agree with God's assessment of ourselves (we're all sinners), judge ourselves worthy of death, and die in repentance. Having died under the curse, we are buried in water, but now by obeying the Law we are made free from the Law—we arise and walk in newness of life. The law of the Spirit of life in Christ Jesus makes us free from the law of sin and death (see Rom. 8:1). It can't get any simpler than that!

Doctrine Four

But wait, what about the fourth column—the feast of Pentecost, the doctrine of laying on of hands, and the corresponding baptism of the Holy Spirit?

Peter said, *"Repent, and be baptized every one of you in the name of Jesus Christ for the remission of sins, and ye shall receive the gift of the Holy Ghost. For the promise is unto you, and to your children, and to all that are afar off, even as many as the Lord our God shall call"* (Acts 2:38-39). Through Peter, God *promised* us the gift of the Holy Spirit as a result of being baptized in Christ's name (see Acts 5:32). It is a perpetual promise to *"as many as the Lord our God shall call."* If you're called, and you've been baptized in His name, the gift is yours for the asking (see Luke 11:13).

Passover	Unleavened Bread	Firstfruits	Pentecost
Repentance	Faith	Baptisms	Laying on Hands
John's Baptism	Good Conscience	Water B.	Holy Spirit

When Paul ran across some of Apollos' converts who didn't have the baptism of the Holy Spirit, he asked them about it. They answered, *"We have not so much as heard whether there be any Holy Ghost."* His immediate response was, *"unto what then were you baptized?"* (Acts 19:2-3). The same problem exists today. Many Christians still haven't been told about the Holy Spirit baptism.

As we learned in Lesson Seven, even a small deviation from the truth produces devious results.

> *And it came to pass, that, while Apollos was at Corinth, Paul having passed through the upper coasts came to Ephesus: and finding certain disciples, He said unto them, Have ye received the Holy Ghost since ye believed? And they said unto him, We have not so much as heard whether there be any Holy Ghost. And he said unto them,* ***Unto what then were ye baptized?*** *And they said, Unto John's baptism.*
>
> *Then said Paul, John verily baptized with the baptism of repentance, saying unto the people, that they should believe on Him which should come after him, that is, on Christ Jesus.* ***When they heard this, they were baptized in the name of the Lord Jesus. And when Paul had laid his hands upon them, the Holy Ghost came on them;*** *and they spake with tongues, and prophesied. And all the men were about twelve* (Acts 19:1-7).

We're supposed to be baptized in the name of Jesus. Paul said, *"whatsoever ye do in word or deed, do all in the name of the Lord Jesus"* (Col. 3:17). The apostles' words and examples make it crystal clear that this commandment includes water baptism (see Acts 2:38; 8:12,16; 10:43,48; 19:5; 22:16). Baptism in Jesus' name also fulfills the commandment of Matthew 28:19:

> *Go ye therefore, and teach all nations, baptizing them in the name of the Father, and of the Son, and of the Holy Ghost.*

As usual, Jesus hid the truth from the wise and prudent by slightly disguising it. He always means exactly what He says, but it's wise to look closely. Sometimes He didn't actually say what we thought He said. This is one of those Scriptures. He said *name* singular, not *titles* plural. What *name* did He mean? He said, *"I come in My Father's name,"* and we know the Son's name is Jesus. Likewise, He said the Father would send the Holy Spirit in His name (see John 5:43; 14:26).

All prayer, all praise, *everything*, including water baptism, should be done in the *name* of the Lord Jesus. His name means Jehovah saves; He is the salvation of Jehovah. Our *spirit* is born again through faith in His name. Our *soul* is saved by calling upon and confessing His name, and our *body* is delivered from the natural ordinances of the Law by baptism in His name.

His death delivered us from the power of death; His resurrection gives us the power of an endless life. Until the very end, the Father has put all things under His authority and the power of His name (see John 1:12; Rom. 10:13, 6:6; Heb. 2:14; 7:16,25; 1 Cor. 15:24-28).

> *Neither is there salvation in any other: for there is none other name under heaven given among men, whereby we must be saved* (Acts 4:12).

As you can see from our previous examination of the Gospel, the fourth column corresponds to the *witness* of Christ's resurrection. Hebrews says, *"The Holy Ghost also is a witness to us..."* (Heb. 10:15), and Jesus said, *"Ye shall receive power, after that the Holy Ghost is come upon you: and ye shall be witnesses unto Me..."* (Acts 1:8). So we see that the Holy Spirit baptism empowers us to witness for Christ.

Likewise, this column contains the feast of Pentecost. When Israel observed this feast in the wilderness, Moses received the Law written on stone. When the early Church observed it in the spirit, they received the Law written in their hearts (see Acts 2:1-4). Paul said all the Law is fulfilled in one word—*love*, and he said *"...the love of God is shed abroad in our hearts by the Holy Ghost which is given unto us"* (Rom. 5:5; see also Gal. 5:14).

God uses the baptism of the Holy Spirit to write His royal law of love upon and within our hearts. Many of His children have never experienced the depth of His love because they haven't experienced this wonderful baptism.

When God visited Israel at Mount Sinai and talked with them, He scared them so badly they asked Moses to stand between them and Him. Moses became their mediator, even as Christ is Mediator for us (see 1 Tim. 2:5).

But, after Moses talked with God for them, he put a veil over his face to symbolize the fact that the truth was hidden from them. Conversely, when Jesus went before God for us, He removed the veil and revealed the truth. The natural ordinances of the Law blinded Israel, but the spirit of the Law *"is a lamp unto my feet, and a light unto my path"* (Ps. 119:105). The spirit of the Law *is* the spirit of truth, which is poured out upon us through the Holy Spirit baptism. The Holy Spirit is the Spirit of revelation itself (see Eph. 1:17). Jesus said:

> *Howbeit when He, the Spirit of truth, is come, He will guide you into all truth: for He shall not speak of Himself; but whatsoever He shall hear, that shall He speak: and He will shew you things to come. He shall glorify Me: for He shall receive of Mine, and shall shew it unto you* (John 16:13-14).

No wonder the devil fights this baptism so hard! But he has even bigger trouble ahead. When John prophesied of the Holy Spirit baptism, he also spoke of another—the baptism of fire:

> *I indeed baptize you with water unto repentance: but He that cometh after me is mightier than I, whose shoes I am not worthy to bear: He shall baptize you with the Holy Ghost, and with fire: Whose fan is in His hand, and He will thoroughly purge His floor, and gather His wheat into the garner; but He will burn up the chaff with unquenchable fire* (Matthew 3:11-12).

Doctrine Five

It's time to ask for the fire—available now:

Passover	Unleavened Bread	Firstfruits	Pentecost	Trumpets
Repentance	Faith	Baptisms	Laying on Hands	Resurrection
John's Baptism	Good Conscience	Water B.	Holy Spirit	Power (Fire)

For the past 100 years, the world has experienced a revived outpouring of the Holy Spirit. Now is the time for the fire to be poured out! Fire is power and purification. Without the power to *"gather His wheat into the garner"* and the cleansing fire to *"purge His floor,"* we'll never be ready for Christ's return. This baptism actually transcends both the fifth and the sixth feasts. The feast of trumpets releases resurrection power, but be ready for the day of atonement. It follows hard on the heels of trumpets.

Doctrine Six

Passover	Unleavened Bread	Firstfruits	Pentecost	Trumpets	Atonement
Repentance	Faith	Baptisms	Hands	Resurrection	Judgment
John's B.	Good Conscience	Water B.	Holy Spirit	Power (Fire)	Purification

> *Also on the tenth day of this seventh month there shall be a day of atonement: it shall be an holy convocation unto you; and ye shall afflict your souls, and offer* ***an offering made by fire*** *unto the Lord....For whatsoever soul it be that shall not be afflicted in that same day, he shall be cut off from among his people* (Leviticus 23:27-29).

The same power that raises the dead will also kill the living. The same anointing that raised the lame man at the gate Beautiful buried Ananias and Sapphira (see Acts 2:3-6; 5:1-11). Judgment's coming, and it begins at the house of God (see 1 Pet. 4:17).

Doctrine Seven

And finally, we come to the last column; the feast of tabernacles, the doctrine of perfection, and the baptism of suffering (or a willing sacrifice; see Matt. 20:22-23):

Passover	Unleavened B.	Firstfruits	Pentecost	Trumpets	Atonement	Tabernacles
Repentance	Faith	Baptisms	Hands	Resurrection	Judgment	Perfection
John's B.	G. Conscience	Water B.	Holy Spirit	Power (Fire)	Purification	Suffering

Many Christians avoid suffering. But it shouldn't be that way. Jesus led the way:

> ***Though He were a Son, yet learned He obedience by the things which He suffered; and being made perfect,*** *He became the author of eternal salvation unto all them that obey Him* (Hebrews 5:8-9).

Paul said, *"For unto you it is given in the behalf of Christ, not only to believe on Him, but also to suffer for His sake"* (Phil. 1:29). Many in our affluent, comfortable, religious society have rejected that aspect of the Gospel. God hasn't, Paul didn't, and we're not supposed to. In fact, Paul implied that we should even look forward to suffering for Christ. He said, I *"rejoice in my sufferings for you, and fill up that which is behind of the afflictions of Christ in my flesh for His body's sake, which is the church"* (Col. 1:24). Why? Because there's an eternal reward for suffering! *"If we suffer* [for Him], *we shall also reign with Him..."* (2 Tim. 2:12).

> *And behold, I am coming quickly; and My reward is with Me, to give every one according to his work* (Revelation 22:12 NKJV).

> *I beseech you therefore, brethren, by the mercies of God, that ye present your bodies a living sacrifice, holy, acceptable unto God, which is your reasonable service. And be not conformed to this world: but be ye transformed by the renewing of your mind, that ye may prove what is that good, and acceptable, and perfect, will of God* (Romans 12:1-2).

ASSIGNMENT: LESSON ELEVEN

1. A. How many different baptisms are there?
   B. Name them.
2. Which baptism saves us?
3. A. Why should we be water baptized?
   B. What does water baptism accomplish in a believer's life?
4. A. What is the proper way to baptize someone?
   B. Who is authorized to perform water baptism?
5. A. Name three things the Holy Spirit baptism accomplishes in a believer's life.
   B. What else does the Bible call the Holy Spirit?

6. A. Which baptism is common to two different feasts and accomplishes two different things?
   B. What are they?
7. Reading assignment: Matthew 5:1–7:29.

Endnote

1. Likewise Christ, and then we through obedience to the Gospel, become "firstfruits" (see 1 Cor. 15:20,23; James 1:18).

LESSON TWELVE

MAGNIFY THE LAW

Isaiah prophesied that when Jesus came He would magnify the Law and make it honorable:

> *The Lord is well pleased for His righteousness' sake; He [His servant Jesus] will magnify the law, and make it honorable* (Isaiah 42:21).

Jesus was the Law in living form. He lived it, fulfilled it, satisfied it, and removed the natural ordinances and commandments it contained. In short, as Isaiah prophesied, He magnified it and made it honorable. When He removed the carnal ordinances through His death on the cross, He released us from the old, natural covenant and established the new covenant through His blood (see Col. 2:14). The old covenant was the Ten Commandments written on tables of stone (see Exod. 34:4,28). The new covenant is Christ's love written on the fleshly tables of our hearts (see Jer. 31:33).

Moses told the Israelites, *"It shall be our righteousness, if we observe to do all these commandments before the Lord our God, as He hath commanded us"* (Deut. 6:25). Of course, they couldn't, and we can't. Our righteousness is by faith, not by our works.

Nevertheless, in spite of that, some of these very same commandments appear to be reinstated in the New Testament.

For example, Deuteronomy 5:16 says, *"Honor thy father and thy mother, as the Lord thy God hath commanded thee; that thy days may be prolonged, and that it may go well with thee, in the land which the Lord thy God giveth thee,"* and Paul, in Ephesians 6:2-3 says, *"Honor thy father and mother; (which is the first commandment with promise;) That it may be well with thee, and thou mayest live long on the earth."*

How are we to reconcile this duplication with our doctrinal understanding of dividing the natural commandments from the spiritual aspects of the Law? One of the first things Jesus told the Jews was:

> *Think not that I am come to destroy the law, or the prophets: I am not come to destroy, but to fulfill. For verily I say unto you, Till heaven and earth pass, one jot or one tittle shall in no wise pass from the law, till all be fulfilled. Whosoever therefore shall break one of these least commandments, and shall teach men so, he shall be called the least in the kingdom of heaven: but whosoever shall do and teach them, the same shall be called great in the kingdom of heaven* (Matthew 5:17-19).

As we have seen, each precept of the law has a spiritual fulfillment—first in Christ, then in His Body, the Church. Under the old covenant, even if a man hated his father or mother, as long as he provided for their material needs he was in full compliance with the Law (see Mark 7:10-12).

Under grace, *honor* takes on a deeper meaning. Instead of emphasizing natural things, it requires us to respect and obey our parents. If they do happen to have material needs, grace requires us to give (see James 2:15-16). But, if we have God's love in our hearts, we are going to automatically do that even without being prompted. This is what Paul meant when he said, *"The righteousness of the law* [is] *fulfilled in us, who walk not after the flesh, but after the Spirit"* (Rom. 8:4).

Each of the Ten Commandments has a spiritual fulfillment which is deeper than the natural. For instance, the Law said, *"Thou shalt not kill"* (Deut. 5:17). Jesus magnified this law when He said, *"Love your enemies, bless them that curse you, do good to them that hate you, and pray for them which despitefully use you, and persecute you"* (Matt. 5:44). Under grace, not only are you forbidden to kill them, you even have to love and pray for them (see Matt. 5:43-44). Jesus also magnified the law condemning adultery. He said:

> *Ye have heard that it was said by them of old time, Thou shalt not commit adultery: But I say unto you, That whosoever looks on a woman to lust after her hath committed adultery with her already in his heart* (Matthew 5:27-28).

In every case, under grace, each commandment takes on a deeper, more spiritual significance. As you can see, obeying the spirit of some laws automatically includes natural compliance. Some don't. Sabbath keeping is one such example. Under the Law, it was a sin to work on the Sabbath day. Under grace, it is a sin to work for God's acceptance on any day of the week. Christ is our Sabbath. He finished His work and is resting. If we are in Christ, we are also resting in His finished work. When we trust in His righteousness instead of our own, we are keeping the Sabbath holy.

When the rich, young ruler came to Jesus for spiritual counsel, he asked what he had to do to obtain eternal life. Jesus replied by quoting several of the Ten Commandments.

> *And, behold, one came and said unto him, Good Master, what good thing shall I do, that I may have eternal life? And He said*

> *unto him...if thou wilt enter into life, keep the commandments. He saith unto Him, Which? Jesus said, Thou shalt do no murder, Thou shalt not commit adultery, Thou shalt not steal, Thou shalt not bear false witness, Honor thy father and thy mother: and, Thou shalt love thy neighbor as thyself* (Matthew 19:16-19).

It's interesting to note that Jesus left out Sabbath keeping, even though under the Law it was emphasized more than any other commandment (see Jer. 17:19-27). Under the old covenant, God promised blessings for keeping it holy, and curses for defiling it:

> *If thou turn away thy foot from the Sabbath, from doing thy pleasure on My holy day; and call the Sabbath a delight, the holy of the Lord, honorable; and shalt honor Him, not doing thine own ways, nor finding thine own pleasure, nor speaking thine own words: Then shalt thou delight thyself in the Lord; and I will cause thee to ride upon the high places of the earth, and feed thee with the heritage of Jacob thy father: for the mouth of the Lord hath spoken it* (Isaiah 58:13-14).

> *Ye shall keep the Sabbath therefore; for it is holy unto you:* ***every one that defiles it shall surely be put to death:*** *for whosoever does any work therein, that soul shall be cut off from among his people* (Exodus 31:14).

> *And while the children of Israel were in the wilderness, they found a man that gathered sticks upon the Sabbath day. And they that found him gathering sticks brought him unto Moses and Aaron.... ...And the Lord said unto Moses, The man shall be surely put to death: all the congregation shall stone him with stones without the camp* (Numbers 15:32-35).

Why was God so adamant about Sabbath keeping? Because He was illustrating that anyone working for his or her salvation is under a curse of death. Salvation simply can't be earned by our righteousness. Working on the Sabbath under the old covenant is the same as working for our salvation under the new. Moses' Law caused bondage. So do all other religious laws, regardless of where they come from.

Legalism is fatal, regardless of whether the laws we obey come from Moses' commandments or from the many holiness laws developed as requirements for salvation by a variety of today's churches. They all defile the Sabbath by replacing faith with works. They all produce self-righteousness instead of the righteousness that is by faith in Christ Jesus, bondage instead of liberty, death instead of life.

> *Christ is become of no effect unto you, whosoever of you are justified by the law; ye are fallen from grace* (Galatians 5:4).

Even Sabbath keeping itself is sin if it is done as a requirement for salvation. A true Christian does good works because he or she is saved, not to get saved, or even to stay saved (see Matt. 5:16; Eph. 2:10). Paul asked, *"Are ye so foolish? having begun in the Spirit, are ye now made perfect by the flesh?"* (Gal. 3:3). You stay saved the same way you get saved—by faith. There's only one Savior, Jesus; and there is only one plan of salvation, the Gospel.

Oddly enough, the Old Testament itself warns against the danger of trying to obtain God's favor through our own efforts, *"Be not righteous over much...why shouldest thou destroy thyself?"* (Eccles. 7:16). And of all places to find a warning against legalism, three times after giving a long list of *thou shalt nots*, Moses said, *"Thou shalt not seethe a kid in his mother's milk"* (Exod. 23:19).

A kid is a baby. It represents a new convert—a new, born-again Christian. Its mother represents the Church, who is the mother of all living. The mother's milk is the Word (see 1 Pet. 2:2). We are not supposed to seethe (boil, i.e., indoctrinate) a newborn Christian in Church doctrine. Or put it another way, Jesus told the legalistic Pharisees, *"Ye compass sea and land to make one proselyte, and when he is made, ye make him twofold more the child of hell than yourselves"* (Matt. 23:15). Jesus is our Savior; the Holy Spirit is our Teacher. God will have it no other way.

> *The grace of the Lord Jesus Christ, and the love of God, and the communion of the Holy Ghost, be with you all* (2 Corinthians 13:14).

ASSIGNMENT: LESSON TWELVE

1. What does it mean to "magnify the Law"?
2. What do the Scriptures compare hatred for one's brother too?
3. A. Is looking at pornography adultery?
   B. Why?
4. A. What happens to people who do not honor their parents?
   B. Is dishonoring parents a violation of the old covenant or the new?
5. A. Which day is a Christian's Sabbath day?
   B. Are Christians required to keep the Jewish Sabbath?
   C. Why, or why not?
6. Under what condition would it be a sin for a Christian to refrain from working on the Sabbath?
7. Reading assignment: Genesis chapters 1–3. Memorize what occurred on each day of creation.

PART II

A PERFECT HEART

I will behave myself wisely in a perfect way. O when wilt Thou come unto me? I will walk within my house with ***a perfect heart*** (Psalm 101:2).

INTRODUCTION

GOD'S BLUEPRINT

In review, there are two primary divisions of the Word of God, the natural and the spiritual. The natural division is essentially the history of the Jews, and it corresponds to the body. The spiritual division is itself divisible into two different levels, one corresponding to the soul, the other to the spirit.

Thus we have three levels of interpretation: body, soul, and spirit. At the risk of over-simplification, we can say that the body level depicts temporal things; the soul level exposes God's conscious thoughts; and, the spirit level reveals His intentions and motives. By examining the Word on all three levels, we gain far more information than we do if we just use one level.

Another, simpler perspective is this; the *literal* interpretation refers to God's purposes as they are fulfilled in the Jewish people, and the spiritual interpretation reveals His purposes as they are fulfilled in and through Christ. They are first fulfilled in the person of Christ (the head); afterward they are fulfilled in His Body, the Church. This is the *Christological* and the *prophetic* levels of interpretation. The Christological revelation refers specifically to Christ, and the prophetic to past, present, and future fulfillment in the Church. When interpreting Scripture, the general rule is *first the natural, then the spiritual* (see 1 Cor. 15:44-46).

> *Chris-tol-o-gy:* 1. The theological study of the person and deeds of Jesus. 2. A doctrine or theory based on Jesus or Jesus' teachings.—Chris'-to-log'i-cal.

In the Old Testament and the Synoptic Gospels, all three levels of division are present simultaneously. For instance, the story about the creation of Adam and Eve is literal. Historically, it happened just as it was recorded in the Bible; Adam was the first man God created, and Eve was the first woman. But Paul revealed the hidden Christological and prophetic mysteries contained in those Scriptures in his epistles—Adam is a type of Christ, who was to follow him, and Eve is a type of the Church, which is the Bride of Christ.

> *And so it is written, The first man Adam was made a living soul; the last Adam was made a quickening spirit. Howbeit that was not first which is spiritual, but that which is natural; and afterward that which is spiritual. The first man is of the earth, earthy: the second Man is the Lord from heaven. As is the earthy, such are they also that are earthy: and as is the heavenly, such are they also that are heavenly. And as we have borne the image of the earthy, we shall also bear the image of the heavenly* (1 Corinthians 15:45-49).

The *Logos*

In Scripture, both God and Christ are called the Word (Greek: *Logos*) of God. *Logos* means "something said (including the thought)...expression." *Logos* is usually used in the sense of a thought that *has been* expressed (for instance, the Scriptures), as opposed to *rhema,* "an utterance, or a thought which *is being* expressed."[1]

Thus, the written Word of God is *Logos*, while a prophetic utterance is *rhema*. Therefore, *a logos* is a thought that has been expressed, but *the Logos* is the Word of God, which is Jesus Christ (see Rev. 19:13).

> *In the beginning was the Word [Logos], and the Word was with God, and the Word was God....And the Word was made flesh, and dwelt among us...* (John 1:1,14).

Jesus *is* the *Logos*. The *Logos "was made flesh, and dwelt among us,"* revealing that even as Jesus had body, soul, and spirit, the living Word of God also has *body* (natural substance and fulfillment), *soul* (conscious thought and action), and *spirit* (life, intent, and purpose). The *body* corresponds to the natural level of interpretation and fulfillment, the *spirit* to the Christological level, and the *soul* to the prophetic fulfillment in the Church.

It is noteworthy that the nature of the natural and spiritual are quite different. In fact, they are reversed and in many ways opposites of one another. For that reason, when interpreting Scripture, the same passage of Scripture can have two very different, yet correct meanings.

> *The heavens declare the glory of God; and the firmament shows His handywork. Day unto day utters speech, and night unto night shows knowledge. There is no speech nor language, where their voice is not heard. Their line is gone out through all the earth, and their words to the end of the world. In them hath He set a tabernacle for the sun* (Psalm 19:1-4).

Visible, natural things reveal invisible, spiritual things. Jesus often used natural events and objects to portray spiritual truth. Likewise, God's natural creation speaks loudly to us from without, revealing His infinite wisdom, His incredible, creative imagination, and even His eternal power and deity (see Rom. 1:20).

Likewise, His Spirit speaks quietly to us from within, through our conscience (the mind of our spirit), revealing even the secret thoughts and intents of His heart—and sometimes even the thoughts of others (see Amos 3:7; 1 Cor. 2:9-12; 14:24-25).

We understand God's nature because He breathed His eternal Spirit into us at creation. Our spirit is *like* His Spirit, and our body is created in His *image*. An image is the reverse of whatever it reflects. When we observe our own image in a mirror, it is reversed (left is right and right is left). This explains the reverse nature of our carnal mind and flesh as compared to our spirit (see Rom. 1:18-20; 2:14-15; 8:6-7).

> *And God said, Let us make man in Our* ***image****, after Our* ***likeness:*** *and let them have dominion over the fish of the sea, and over the fowl of the air, and over the cattle, and over all the earth, and over every creeping thing that creeps upon the earth* (Genesis 1:26).

Image means: "shade, a phantom i.e., (figurative) illusion, resemblance," and *likeness* means: "resemblance, concrete model, shape, adverb like."[2]

God's Disclaimer

> *These are the generations of the heavens and of the earth when they were created, in the day that the Lord God made the earth and the heavens, And every plant of the field* ***before it was in the earth,*** *and every herb of the field before it grew: for the Lord God had not caused it to rain upon the earth,* ***and there was not a man to till the ground*** (Genesis 2:4-5).

Although the first chapter of Genesis details the creation of the heavens and the earth and all living things contained therein, including man, Genesis 2:4-5 reveals that chapter 1 doesn't tell the whole story. It says that God made man and then chapter 2 adds that He rested when He was finished, but the disclaimer in Genesis 2:4-5 reveals that both statements are prophetic.

> *...God...quickeneth the dead, and calleth those things which be not as though they were* (Romans 4:17).

God's Blueprint

God predetermined all that He was going to do before He started creating anything. His Word is His will, and His will is the blueprint that all things must conform to before it is acceptable to Him. He has completed His work in the heavens, but in the earth He is *actively* working out His will even now.

> *In whom also we have obtained an inheritance, being predestinated according to the purpose of Him* ***who works all things after the counsel of His own will*** (Ephesians 1:11).

The word *works* in this passage means "to be active...."[3] Jesus said to pray, *"Thy kingdom come. Thy will be done in earth, as it is in heaven"* (Matt. 6:10). His will still has to *be* done (completed) in earth, but it *is* done (complete) in Heaven. When He speaks, it is from a heavenly perspective, not an earthly one. He *"calleth those things which be not as though they were"* (Rom. 4:17).

So, when you read that He made or completed something, look closely—it could be that He hasn't even started it yet. The following two Scriptures that we are discussing are good examples!

> *And God said, Let Us make man in Our image, after Our likeness: and let them have dominion over the fish of the sea,*

and over the fowl of the air, and over the cattle, and over all the earth, and over every creeping thing that creeps upon the earth. So God created man in His own image, ***in the image of God created He him; male and female created He them*** (Genesis 1:26-27).

And on the seventh day God ended His work which He had made; ***and He rested on the seventh day from all His work which He had made*** (Genesis 2:2).

But as we've already seen, in the earth, He's neither finished nor resting. His disclaimer, *"and there was not a man to till the ground"* in Genesis 2:5 reveals that, although His work was completed in Heaven, He was just beginning the process of creation on earth. And He's still making us into His own image and likeness even unto this very day.

Everyone He saves is predestined to be conformed to the image of His son (see Rom. 8:29). This is accomplished through the ministry of the Holy Spirit and the teaching and preaching of the Word of God.

The Bible says, *"Known unto God are all His works from the beginning of the world,"* and in Heaven, God's *"works were finished from the foundation of the world,"* but on earth, He's still working out His blueprint with and through *us* as we preach His Word and proclaim the Gospel (see Acts 15:18; Heb. 4:3). Paul said, *"We are laborers together with God"* (1 Cor. 3:9). In other words, *God's plan* is complete in Heaven, and *Christ's work* is finished on earth, but God really won't rest until *we* finish publishing the Gospel to all the world, making disciples of all peoples in every nation. Therefore God's "us" and "our" in Genesis 1:26-27 includes both Christ *and* the Church in the continuing process of humankind's creation into His image and likeness.

> *Heaven is My throne, and earth is My footstool: what house will ye build Me? saith the Lord: or* ***what is the place of My rest?*** (Acts 7:49)

Of course the answer to that question is *the Church.* The Church is God's house. Paul said that we *"are God's building"* (see 1 Cor. 3:9; Heb. 3:6; 2 Pet. 3:8; Rev. 20:2). When His house is completed, Jesus will return and set up His millennium Kingdom. The millennium is the seventh day of creation. It is a time of rest for both God and humankind because there will be no war, natural or spiritual. Satan will be bound for the whole day (1,000 years), and Christ will rule the earth in peace.

Generational Theology

> *These are the* ***generations*** *of the heavens and of the earth when they were created, in the day that the Lord God made the earth and the heavens* (Genesis 2:4).

Here, the word *generations* means "descent."[4]

God's blueprint includes *four generations* of the heavens and the earth, covered by the seven days of creation enumerated in Genesis 1:1-2:4 (also see Gen. 15:13-16; Num. 14:18; Deut. 23:7-8; Matt. 24:33-34; 1 Pet. 2:9).

The first is the *generation of Innocence.* After Adam's fall, although sin was in the world, it was not imputed unto humanity (see Rom. 5:13). The presence of sin generated the need for *Law,* that sin might become exceedingly sinful (see Rom. 7:13). But once the Law was given, it condemned all humankind, generating the need for *grace.*

Under grace, God is completing His plan and fulfilling His purpose to bring many sons and daughters into glory (see Heb. 2:10). All who accept His abundant grace by obeying the Gospel will be rewarded for their obedience. Thus, grace generates the need for *reward*, which will be fulfilled in the millennium Kingdom (see Rev. 22:12).

Endnotes

1. James Strong, *Strong's Exhaustive Concordance*, Greek #3056, 4487.
2. Strong, Hebrew #6754, 1823.
3. Strong, Greek #1754.
4. Strong, Hebrew #8434.

DAY ONE

THE MAN OF SIN

In the beginning God created the heaven and the earth. And the earth was without form, and void; and ***darkness was upon the face of the deep.*** *And the Spirit of God moved upon the face of the waters. And God said, Let there be light: and there was light. And God saw the light, that it was good: and God divided the light from the darkness. And God called the light Day, and the darkness He called Night. And the evening and the morning were the first day* (Genesis 1:1-5).

In this passage, the phrase translated *without form* means "waste (land), a desolation, desert, worthless." *Void* means "empty," and *moved* means "to brood."[1]

First column of precepts	Feast of Passover
	Doctrine of Repentance
	Baptism of Repentance
	First light–earth void

Ever since the fall of Adam, humankind in our natural state is lost. We are sinners by nature. Although we have the potential of godliness in our spirits, our flesh is weak (see Matt. 26:41). We are *without form* and *void.* That is, we are not *like* God in His thoughts and actions, and we are *void* of wisdom and the fear of God (see Rom. 3:10-18; Ps. 10:4).

> *The first man is of the earth,* ***earthy****: the second Man is the Lord from heaven* (1 Corinthians 15:47).

The word *earthy* means "dusty or dirty, a heap of rubbish."[2]

Although God made humankind without form and void, He had no intention of leaving us that way. As we have already seen, from the beginning God's stated purpose was to *"bring many sons into glory."* Every person who receives Christ is predestined to be conformed to the image of His Son. Under Moses' Law, people couldn't look upon God's face (our face reveals our heart) because *"darkness was upon the face of the deep."* But God had the solution worked out before He even created the problem.

> *For God, who commanded the light to shine out of darkness, hath shined in our hearts, to give the light of the knowledge of the glory of God in the* ***face*** *of Jesus Christ* (2 Corinthians 4:6).

God sent forth His Son into the world that the world through Him might have, *"the light of the knowledge of* [the deep things] *of God."* Jesus is the spiritual light that God spoke into existence on the very first day of creation. Jesus was the intended Light of the world before the natural sun was ever created (see John 1:3-4; 8:12).

Jesus *is* light. The Bible says that His Word is *"a lamp unto my feet, and a light unto my path"* (Ps. 119:105). Because Jesus is the Word, every Scripture in some way reveals Christ. As we discovered earlier, some Scriptures reveal His divine nature; some His supernatural attributes; some His humanity; some His judgments; some His office and work; and some, His heart. For example:

> [A eunuch] *was returning* [from Jerusalem]. *And sitting in his chariot, he was reading Isaiah the prophet. Then the Spirit said to Philip, "Go near and overtake this chariot." So Philip ran to him, and heard him reading the prophet Isaiah, and said, "Do you understand what you are reading?" And he said, "How can I, unless someone guides me?" And he asked Philip to come up and sit with him. The place in the Scripture which he read was this: "He was led as a sheep to the slaughter; and as a lamb before its shearer is silent, so He opened not His mouth. In His humiliation His justice was taken away, And who will declare His generation? For His life is taken from the earth."*
>
> *So the eunuch answered Philip and said, "I ask you, of whom does the prophet say this, of himself or of some other man?"* ***Then Philip opened his mouth, and beginning at this Scripture, preached Jesus to him*** (Acts 8:28-35 NKJV).

When Phillip answered the eunuch, he didn't have to turn to Moses' writings or some other Scripture to show him Christ; he simply preached Christ from where he was already reading, because every Scripture declares Him. For example, compare Deuteronomy 30:11-14 with Romans 10:5-8. Since the Church is Christ's Body, hidden right within each Scripture lies both the mystery of Christ and the Church.

Thus, the *literal* interpretation of Genesis 1:1-5 is seen by simply looking around. Heaven and earth are the works of God's hands. But, as Paul revealed in Second Corinthians 4:6, the *Christological* interpretation is seen in these very same verses of Scripture. Likewise, the *prophetic* interpretation discloses the beginning of the Church there.

The Holy Spirit brooded on the face of the waters (*seas*, i.e., multitudes) to bring people unto Himself. This interpretation of the "waters" is confirmed in one of Isaiah's prophesies:

Then thou shalt see, and flow together, and thine heart shall fear, and be enlarged; because ***the abundance of the sea shall be converted unto thee, the forces of the Gentiles shall come unto thee*** (Isaiah 60:5).

Thus, from Genesis 1:1-5 we can see that it is God who takes the first step in the conversion of people. One means *beginning*. It all starts with Him. *"We love Him because He first loved us"* (1 John 4:19). Although it is up to people to respond to God's Spirit dealing with them, without the Spirit's drawing, they have nothing to respond to except their own carnal passions and lust.

[Jesus said] *No man can come to Me, except the Father which hath sent Me draw him...* (John 6:44).

Endnotes

1. James Strong, *Strong's Exhaustive Concordance,* Hebrew #8414, 922, 7363.
2. Strong, Greek #5517.

DAY TWO

THE SPIRITUAL MIND

In the beginning God created the heaven and the earth.... And God said, Let there be a ***firmament*** *in the midst of the waters, and let it divide the waters from the waters. And God made the firmament, and divided the waters which were under the firmament from the waters which were above the firmament: and it was so. And God called the firmament Heaven. And the evening and the morning were the second day* (Genesis 1:1,6-8).

The Hebrew word in this passage for *firmament* means "an expanse (pounded out)."[1]

Second Column of Precepts	Feast of Unleavened Bread
	Doctrine of Faith Toward God
	Baptism of Faith (good conscience)
	The second heaven created

When the Holy Spirit "broods" over our spirits and speaks light into our hearts, He convicts us of sin. This is seen in the second act of creation, when God for the second time made a heaven and then vertically divided the earth's water.

God created the first heaven on the first day and the second heaven on the second day. In addition to these two heavens, the Bible tells us that at some point He also made a third heaven. Paul had an experience where he talks about it, which he also called paradise.

> *I knew a man in Christ about fourteen years ago, (whether in the body, I cannot tell; or whether out of the body, I cannot tell: God knows;) such an one* ***caught up to the third heaven.*** *And I knew such a man, (whether in the body, or out of the body, I cannot tell: God knows;) how that* ***he was caught up into paradise,*** *and heard unspeakable words, which it is not lawful for a man to utter* (2 Corinthians 12:2-4).

Jesus referred to paradise (the third heaven) when He promised the thief on the cross that he would be with Him the same day they died.

> *And he said unto Jesus, Lord, remember Me when Thou comest into Thy kingdom. And Jesus said unto him, Verily I say unto thee,* ***To day shalt thou be with Me in paradise*** (Luke 23:42-43).

The first, natural heaven includes the entire universe; the second heaven is in "the midst of the waters," and in the natural it corresponds to earth's atmosphere. The spiritual interpretation of the second heaven is the mind of humans. Obviously, there is perfect peace in the third heaven, but even as humankind wars in the flesh in the first heaven, Revelation 12:7 reveals there is spiritual war in the second heaven. This war is fought in our conscious minds or souls.

In the beginning, Adam was given full authority over all the works of God's hands. He was made "the god of this world," and the "prince of the power of the air." He was king, and the world was his kingdom. When he submitted himself to satan,

satan became his head and obtained the power that God had entrusted to him, and the glorious kingdom that God created for humankind became the "kingdom of darkness," instead. Thus, satan became "the prince of the power of the air" instead of Adam.

> *Wherein in time past ye walked according to the course of this world, according to* ***the prince of the power of the air,*** *the spirit that now worketh in the children of disobedience* (Ephesians 2:2).

> *For we wrestle not against flesh and blood, but against principalities, against powers, against the rulers of the darkness of this world, against spiritual wickedness in high places* (Ephesians 6:12).

When Jesus defeated satan, He gained back all the power that Adam lost, thus reclaiming the title and position of *"God of this world"* for humankind (2 Cor. 4:4). Although He is the King, and all power and authority are His, He is still in the process of putting down the rebellion from hell that started the downfall of Adam's kingdom. The Kingdom that He is establishing is not *of* this world, even though it is *in* this world. This world is temporary. The King is eternal, and of His Kingdom there will be no end!

> *And He shall reign over the house of Jacob for ever; and of His kingdom there shall be no end* (Luke 1:33).

The war to end all wars is being fought in people's hearts. The spiritual mind wars against the carnal (see Gal. 5:17). The mind of Christ is continually warring against the carnal mind of all people. A person's mind is like a garden. The lowly, earthy, sensual thoughts (seed) that satan plants bring forth death. The pure, heavenly thoughts (seed) of Christ's Word and Spirit produce life and peace.

> *But if ye have bitter envying and strife in your hearts, glory not, and lie not against the truth.* ***This wisdom descends not from above, but is earthly, sensual, devilish.*** *For where envying and strife is, there is confusion and every evil work. But the wisdom that is from above is first pure, then peaceable, gentle, and easy to be entreated, full of mercy and good fruits, without partiality, and without hypocrisy* (James 3:14-17).

Weed the Garden

The first work of the Holy Spirit is to weed the garden. He must convict our hearts so that we will no longer think as the world does. He separates our lowly, carnal thoughts from the lofty, heavenly thoughts that spring up from our spirits. He transforms us through our minds, by His Spirit (see John 16:7-11).

> *And be not conformed to this world: but* ***be ye transformed by the renewing of your mind,*** *that ye may prove what is that good, and acceptable, and perfect, will of God* (Romans 12:2).

Thus, day by day God is making the firmament. The second heaven is still being "pounded out." Each person, through the continual working of His Spirit, is being transformed into the image of the King. Each citizen of His Kingdom is expected to war against satan with Christ until He has completely conquered all. The rebellion that began in the mind of Eve so long ago will one day be completely quelled. The earth will be filled with the knowledge of the glory of the Lord as the waters cover the sea (see Isa. 11:9; Hab. 2:14).

If we agree with and walk after the course of this world, we die. But, if through the conviction and power of the Holy Spirit we agree with God and walk in the Spirit as citizens of the Kingdom of Heaven, we have eternal life. Our thoughts lead the way.

> *Hear, O earth: behold,* ***I will bring evil upon this people, even the fruit of their thoughts,*** *because they have not hearkened unto My words, nor to My law, but rejected it* (Jeremiah 6:19).

Satan's primary *distraction* to prevent us from thinking about the precious, eternal things of Heaven, and *attraction* to lure us into his snare, is the *things* of the world. We cannot *be* like Christ until we *think* like Christ. As a man *"thinketh in his heart, so is he"* (Prov. 23:7). Our treasures dictate our thoughts. Jesus said, *"Where your treasure is, there will your heart be also"* (Matt. 6:21). Paul said, *"Set your affection on things above, not on things on the earth"* (Col. 3:2).

We cannot be like Him until we think like Him. We cannot think like Him until we learn to love what He loves and only what He loves. He said, *"Ye are they which justify yourselves before men; but God knows your hearts: for that which is highly esteemed among men is abomination in the sight of God"* (Luke 16:15). Be not deceived; whatever we continually think about is what we love. It doesn't matter what it is; as long as it is of this world, it is temporary, and it is hindering us from thinking about Him.

> *Love not the world, neither the things that are in the world. If any man love the world, the love of the Father is not in him. For all that is in the world, the lust of the flesh, and the lust of the eyes, and the pride of life, is not of the Father, but is of the world. And the world passeth away, and the lust thereof: but he that doeth the will of God abideth for ever* (1 John 2:15-17).

Two means "to divide or judge." We must allow His righteous Spirit to divide our thoughts and choose the good and shun the evil.

> *For they that are after the flesh do mind the things of the flesh; but they that are after the Spirit the* ***things*** *of the Spirit. For to be carnally minded is death; but to be spiritually minded is life and peace* (Romans 8:5-6).

Endnote

1. James Strong, *Strong's Exhaustive Concordance,* Hebrew #7548, 7554.

DAY THREE

CONVICTED AND ASHAMED

And God said, Let the waters under the heaven be gathered together unto one place, and let the ***dry*** *land appear: and it was so. And God called the dry land Earth; and the gathering together of the waters called He Seas: and God saw that it was good. And God said, Let the earth bring forth grass, the herb yielding seed, and the fruit tree yielding fruit after his kind, whose seed is in itself, upon the earth: and it was so. And the earth brought forth grass, and herb yielding seed after his kind, and the tree yielding fruit, whose seed was in itself, after his kind: and God saw that it was good. And the evening and the morning were the third day* (Genesis 1:9-13).

The phrase translated as, *dry ground* means "to be ashamed, confused or disappointed."[1]

Third Column of Precepts Feast of Firstfruits
Doctrine of Baptisms
Water baptism
Dry land revealed

The conviction of the Holy Spirit divides our spiritual thoughts from our carnal, lustful desires. The knowledge of sin brings shame. Before a man continues in sin, he first subdues his conscience, which is the mind of his spirit. He covers himself with self-justifying thoughts. The Holy Spirit exposes those thoughts for what they really are, excuses to rebel against God's commandments. Once a man's heart is fully exposed, he becomes ashamed and repents. He will not change as long as his heart is covered (see Deut. 10:16). He must be convicted of his sin. He has to be made ashamed of his former thoughts and conduct.

> *For when ye were the servants of sin, ye were free from righteousness.* ***What fruit had ye then in those things whereof ye are now ashamed?*** *for the end of those things is death* (Romans 6:20-21).

> *For godly sorrow works repentance to salvation not to be repented of: but the sorrow of the world works death. For behold this selfsame thing, that ye sorrowed after a godly sort, what carefulness it wrought in you, yea, what clearing of yourselves, yea, what indignation, yea, what fear, yea, what vehement desire, yea, what zeal, yea, what revenge! In all things ye have approved yourselves to be clear in this matter* (2 Corinthians 7:10-11).

Conviction is one of the primary works of the Holy Spirit. That's the reason He's not welcomed into many churches today. You can't ordain homosexuals with His approval. You can't commit fornication in any manner and esteem yourself righteous without first covering yourself with the self-serving waters of self-justification. Jesus said, *"I will send Him* [the Comforter] *unto you. And when He is come, He will reprove the world of sin, and of righteousness, and of judgment"* (John 16:7-8). The wet land of our souls, left to itself, will bring forth only briers and thorns. God brings forth eternal fruit from well-drained, dry land. It must first be ashamed of itself and dried up from all selfishness, self-justification, and self-righteousness before His seed will prosper.

In nature, every seed produces after its own kind. This is the first scriptural correction to humankind's doctrine of evolution. The same holds true in the spirit. Humanity's word is temporal, and so is its fruit. Those who sow to their flesh shall of the flesh reap corruption (see Gal. 6:8). It cannot be otherwise. God's Word is eternal. It is the only thing that can bring forth the fruit of eternal life. Jesus is the only eternal Seed that God made. All others are temporal:

> *Now to Abraham and his Seed were the promises made. He saith not, And to seeds, as of many; but as of one, And to thy Seed, which is Christ* (Galatians 3:16).

> *That thou keep this commandment without spot, unrebukeable, until the appearing of our Lord Jesus Christ: Which in His times He shall shew, who is the blessed and only Potentate, the King of kings, and Lord of lords;* ***Who only hath immortality,*** *dwelling in the light which no man can approach unto; whom no man hath seen, nor can see: to whom be honor and power everlasting. Amen* (1 Timothy 6:14-16).

Only those who are *in* Christ have eternal life. If you are not a member of His glorious Body, you are lost. If Jesus is not your Lord, and unless His life *is* your life, you are dead while you live. *"But she that liveth in pleasure is dead while she liveth"* (1 Tim. 5:6).

> *And when He had called the people unto Him with His disciples also, He said unto them, Whosoever will come after Me, let him deny himself, and take up his cross, and follow Me.* ***For whosoever will save his life shall lose it;*** *but whosoever shall lose his life for My sake and the gospel's, the same shall save it.*

For what shall it profit a man, if he shall gain the whole world, and lose his own soul? (Mark 8:34-36)

If any man come to Me, and hate not his father, and mother, and wife, and children, and brethren, and sisters, yea, ***and his own life also,*** *he cannot be My disciple. And whosoever doth not bear his cross, and come after Me, cannot be My disciple* (Luke 14:26-27).

Three means to *conform.*[2] God knew us all from the beginning. Those *"He did foreknow, He also did predestinate to be conformed to the image of His Son, that He might be the firstborn among many brethren"* (Rom. 8:29). When our lives conform to His, we become exceedingly fruitful.

If ye abide in Me, and My words abide in you, ye shall ask what ye will, and it shall be done unto you. Herein is My Father glorified, that ye bear much fruit; so shall ye be My disciples (John 15:7-8).

Endnotes

1. James Strong, *Strong's Exhaustive Concordance,* Hebrew #3004, 3001.
2. Ira Milligan, *Understanding the Dreams You Dream, Vol. II* (Shippensburg, PA: Destiny Image, 2010), 7.

DAY FOUR

DOMINION OVER DARKNESS

And God said, Let there be lights in the firmament of the heaven to divide the day from the night; and let them be for signs, and for seasons, and for days, and years: And let them be for lights in the firmament of the heaven to give light upon the earth: and it was so. And God made two great lights; the greater light to rule the day, and the lesser light to rule the night: He made the stars also. And God set them in the firmament of the heaven to give light upon the earth, and ***to rule over the day and over the night, and to divide the light from the darkness:*** *and God saw that it was good. And the evening and the morning were the fourth day* (Genesis 1:14-19).

In this passage, the Hebrew word *signs* means "signal, as a flag, beacon, monument, omen, prodigy, evidence."[1]

Fourth Column of Precepts: Feast of Pentecost
Doctrine of Laying on of Hands
Baptism of the Holy Spirit
Sun, moon, and stars

This Scripture from Genesis 1:14-19 gives us the historical record of the creation of the sun, moon, and stars. God wants us to know that He made them all (see Ps. 8:3). But obviously, that's not His primary reason for stating that fact here, because He already has grass and fruit trees growing and producing fruit in day three. Fruit trees won't even grow in the shade, much less on an earth without sunlight. It may come as a shock to some, but the seven days of creation are not in chronological order—*they are in spiritual order!*

Christ is the greater Light that was made to rule the day, and the Church is the lesser light made to rule the night. Likewise, those who turn many to righteousness were made to shine as the stars forever and ever (see Dan. 12:3).

During the first three "days" of our spiritual journey, God prepares us for His service (see Exod. 3:16-18; 8:27; 15:22-25). After *"casting down* [logical reasoning and] *imaginations, and every high thing that exalts itself against the knowledge of God, and bringing into captivity every thought to the obedience of Christ,"* we are commanded to have within ourselves *"a readiness to revenge all disobedience, when* [our] *obedience is fulfilled"* (2 Cor. 10:5-6). Without the sanctification experiences of the second and third day, we are unqualified to work with Christ for God.[2] *"...be ye clean, that bear the vessels of the Lord"* (Isa. 52:11).

The Holy Spirit first moves upon us, then works through us. First we are drawn by the Spirit, then judged and justified by faith in the finished work of Christ. Next we are separated from the Law through baptism in His name. Then our spirits are joined with His (see 1 Cor. 6:17). This is accomplished through the baptism of the Holy Spirit. He fills us with His Spirit so that we can be partakers of His glory. At this point, corporately, we are as the moon. The moon has no atmosphere or light of its own. Likewise, the Church sits in heavenly places, basking in the light of the Son, reflecting it into a dark and troubled world (see Eph. 2:6).

Individually, we are stars. In the beginning we were without form and void, and darkness was upon the face of the deep. We couldn't understand our own deep thoughts, much less God's (see Jer. 17:9). But now we are *"light in the Lord";* and like the sons of Jacob, we each shine with a light of our own (see Eph. 5:8; Gen. 37:9-10).

Once our thoughts align with His and our lives become fruitful through obedience, God baptizes us with His Spirit so that we can work with Him to fulfill His purpose in us. In other words, on day four, He drafts us into His army to subdue the very same rebellion that we participated in before we were saved.

Christ is the Light of the world. His light is administered through the Spirit. The manifestation of the Spirit equips us to speak as Christ spoke, know as He knew, and do the works that He did. Jesus said, "*...He that believeth on Me, the works that I do shall he do also; and greater works than these shall he do...*" (John 14:12).

Part of our spiritual heritage is to walk in supernatural manifestations. Through the baptism of the Holy Spirit, we can speak for Him through messages in other tongues, along with their interpretation, or through prophecy. His Spirit enables us to know the secrets of people's hearts to confirm His presence in us (see 1 Cor. 14:24-25).

And last, He empowers us to heal and do wonders to convince the world of the truth of the Gospel (see Mark 16:17-18). Paul said that he ministered in supernatural power so that his converts' faith wouldn't stand in the wisdom of men, but in the power of God! (See First Corinthians 2:4-5.) Intellectual faith is easily shaken. Holy Ghost faith shakes the world.

Many Christians forego the baptism of the Holy Spirit, not realizing what He can do for them. They haven't been taught that the Spirit of truth will guide them into all truth; the Spirit of holiness will separate them from this world; the Spirit of adoption will continually give them assurance of their acceptance in the beloved; the Spirit of wisdom and revelation will open the eyes of their understanding into the depths of the mysteries of God's Kingdom; and the Spirit of grace will enable them to both speak and work for God (see John 14:17; Rom. 1:4, 8:15; Eph. 1:5-6,17-20; Heb. 10:29; Rev. 19:10; 1 Pet. 4:10-11). We can do very little without Him. Even Jesus didn't begin His ministry until He was baptized in the Spirit (see John 1:32-33; Luke 3:21-22; 4:1,14,18-19). It is wise to follow in His footsteps.

Four means "rule"[3] or dominion and often includes the subject that is ruled over. Thus it symbolizes both the King and the Kingdom. We've been commissioned to rule. We must use our God-given authority and exercise dominion over this present darkness.

> *For ye were sometimes darkness, but now are ye light in the Lord: walk as children of light...And have no fellowship with the unfruitful works of darkness, but rather reprove them. For...all things that are reproved are made manifest by the light: for whatsoever doth make manifest is light. Wherefore He saith, Awake thou that sleepest, and* ***arise from the dead****, and Christ shall give thee light* (Ephesians 5:8-14).

Arise indeed, for that is the subject of the fifth day.

Endnotes

1. James Strong, *Strong's Exhaustive Concordance,* Hebrew #226.
2. It is important to understand that we aren't sanctified by our works, but through faith in Christ (see Acts 26:18).
3. Ira Milligan, *Understanding the Dreams You Dream, Volume II* (Shippensburg, PA: Destiny Image, 2010), 7.

DAY FIVE

PURE MOTIVES, LIVING WORDS

And God said, Let the waters bring forth abundantly the moving creature that hath life, and fowl that may fly above the earth in the open firmament of heaven. And God created great whales, and every living creature that moves, which the waters brought forth abundantly, after their kind, and every winged fowl after his kind: and God saw that it was good. And God blessed them, saying, ***Be fruitful, and multiply****, and fill the waters in the seas, and let fowl multiply in the earth. And the evening and the morning were the fifth day* (Genesis 1:20-23).

Fifth Column of Precepts	Feast of Trumpets Doctrine of Resurrection of the dead Baptism of Fire (power) Waters bring forth life

As we've already seen, the Law is spiritual. The record of God's natural works is to reveal spiritual truth, not to disprove evolution or prove creationism. In fact, the Scriptures' natural record of creation agrees at least in part with the evolutionary theory of the origin of life—saying it all began in water. The difference is that evolutionists say it all happened by chance, and God said *He* made it happen.

God is invisible. If Christians watched God make life, they would give God credit because they would understand, *"through faith...that things which are seen were not made of things which do appear"* (Heb. 11:3). On the other hand, if evolutionist scientists watched God make life, they would wonder why it happened, and then try to explain what they saw through natural reasoning.

Paul said that when science opposes Scripture, the error is in science's *interpretation* of the data, not in the data itself:

> *O Timothy, keep that which is committed to thy trust, avoiding profane and vain babblings, and oppositions of science* ***falsely so called*** (1 Timothy 6:20).

In the case of the origin of animal life, evolutionist scientists rightly say it all started in water. But, as already pointed out, they are in error as to how and why it took place. Also as mentioned, they ignore the daily testimony that is all around them—every seed produces after its own kind. Both Scripture and nature are adamant about that (see Gen. 1:11-12). Mice cannot produce elephants. Cats cannot breed with dogs. God made each individual species, just like He said He did. But as we've already seen, there's a lot more to the scriptural record of His creation than meets the evolutionist scientists' eye.

The Bible is a spiritual book, written for spiritually-minded people. The world by wisdom knows not God, and many Christians really don't know Him very well either (see 1 Cor. 1:21). Carnally-minded Christians aren't doing God or themselves a favor when they feud with science over the theory of evolution.[1] The Bible and the earth agree. It is an error to say that one opposes the other. Both must be interpreted by the Word of God, and neither say what most people think they say.

Why then, if not to disprove the theory of evolution, did God give us the record of the fifth day? What spiritual truth is hidden in the natural creation of the birds of the air and the creatures of the deep? To help find the answer, let's take another look at our fifth column of precepts:

The Feast of Trumpets
The Doctrine of the Resurrection of the dead
The Baptism of Fire (power)
The Waters bring forth life

In the Scriptures, birds and fish often portray both people and spirits at one time or another. Christ used "fish" to symbolize both people and the Holy Spirit (see Luke 11:11-13; Mark 1:17). Sometimes birds and fish are even more subtle, depicting people's thoughts and words or even the motives of their hearts (see Eccles. 9:12; Matt. 13:4,19):

> *As a cage is full of birds, so are their houses full of deceit: therefore they are become great, and waxen rich* (Jeremiah 5:27).

> *Curse not the king, no not in thy thought; and curse not the rich in thy bedchamber: for a bird of the air shall carry the voice, and that which hath wings shall tell the matter* (Ecclesiastes 10:20).

Jesus said we can do nothing of ourselves. If that be so, and it is, then before we can accomplish much of anything, God has to impart both His motives and His words to us. As we yield to the inspiration of His Spirit, the waters of our spirits release His words to bring forth life upon the earth. The fish correspond to the love of God moving and working within our spirits and the groaning of the Holy Spirit within our souls. The birds depict the anointed word of God. Jesus said, *"It is the Spirit that quickens; the flesh profits nothing: the words that I speak unto you, they are spirit, and they are life"* (John 6:63).

When we believe in our hearts and speak with our mouths, His creative, life-giving resurrection power is released (see Mark 11:22-23). We've seen a little. We will soon experience a mighty explosion of the Creator's supernatural power working to bring forth life in the earth:

> *Verily, verily, I say unto you, The hour is coming, and now is, when the dead shall hear the voice of the Son of God: and they that hear shall live. For as the Father hath life in Himself; so hath He given to the Son to have life in Himself; and hath given Him authority to execute judgment also, because He is the Son of man* (John 5:25-27).

Paul prayed for the Ephesians to receive the Spirit of wisdom and revelation so they would know, "*...the exceeding greatness of His power to us-ward who believe, according to the working of His mighty power, which He wrought in Christ, when He raised Him from the dead...*" (Eph. 1:19-20). The whole Church should continue Paul's prayer.

Five means "service or work."[2] Soon we'll be able to do just that. The works Jesus did, we shall do also. The fifth day is dawning over the horizon of time even now. The trumpets are beginning to sound.

The feast of trumpets is the first feast of the third gathering of Israel (see Deut. 16:16). The first gathering celebrated Israel's exodus from Egypt. The spiritual fulfillment is when we repent and turn wholeheartedly to God.

The second culminated at Mount Sinai, where Moses received the Law. It is fulfilled when God writes His Law on the fleshly tables of our hearts.

The third took place each year when Israel gathered in the year-end harvest. The spiritual fulfillment is soon to come.

> *Be patient therefore, brethren, unto the coming of the Lord. Behold, the husbandman waits for the precious fruit of the earth, and hath long patience for it, until he receive the early and latter rain. Be ye also patient; establish your hearts: for the coming of the Lord draws nigh* (James 5:7-8).

Endnotes

1. I'm not saying that I agree with the theory of evolution. I'm saying that some modern scientists have changed their views concerning the origin of life, and these views are very close to the Genesis explanation of creation. See Alan Hayward, *Creation and Evolution, Rethinking the Evidence from Science and the Bible* (Grand Rapids, MI: Bethany House Publishers, 1985).
2. Ira Milligan, *Understanding the Dreams You Dream, Vol. II* (Shippensburg, PA: Destiny Image, 2010), 8.

DAY SIX

THE IMAGE OF GOD

And God said, Let the earth bring forth the living creature after his kind, cattle, and creeping thing, and beast of the earth after his kind: and it was so. And God made the beast of the earth after his kind, and cattle after their kind, and every thing that creeps upon the earth after his kind....

And God said, Let Us make man in Our ***image****, after Our* ***likeness****: and let them have dominion over the fish of the sea, and over the fowl of the air, and over the cattle, and over all the earth, and over every creeping thing that creeps upon the earth. So God created man in His own* ***image****, in the image of God created He him; male and female created He them. And God blessed them, and God said unto them, Be fruitful, and multiply, and replenish the earth, and subdue it: and have dominion over the fish of the sea, and over the fowl of the air, and over every living thing that moves upon the earth....And God saw every thing that He had made, and, behold, it was very good. And the evening and the morning were the sixth day* (Genesis 1:24-31).

The Hebrew word for *image* means "shade, a phantom i.e., (figurative) illusion, resemblance," and *likeness* means "resemblance, concrete model, shape, adverb: like."[1]

Sixth Column of Precepts Feast of the Day of Atonement
Doctrine of Eternal Judgment
Baptism of Fire (purification)
The image of God

God forbade people to make any image or likeness of Himself or of any god on the face of the earth. The only image to be made was made by God Himself. He created people in His own image and likeness. As discussed previously, God's image is the flesh of people. His likeness is the human spirit. The fleshly, natural image was created first; the pure and innocent spirit was made second.

The flesh is like satan, God's exact opposite. The spirit is in perfect harmony with God. Thus humanity is a paradox. We have the potential to be like God, but because of the weakness of our flesh, we forever fall short of fulfilling that potential. Paul said, *"all have sinned, and come short of the glory of God"* (Rom. 3:23). And indeed, we have.

We are co-laborers with God in the continual creation of people into His image and likeness. In the *natural,* each new birth brings forth another person in His image, which is our likeness. In the *spiritual,* each new birth brings forth another person into His likeness, which is our image. We, God and people, are continually making people in our likeness and our image! (See Genesis 1:26.)

Solomon said that God made people upright, but that people had invented many (evil) inventions (see Eccles. 7:29). Although God created a perfect humanity, it wasn't long until satan took advantage of humanity's basic, carnal nature and drew the first humans into sin. To understand this better, we need to take a closer look at all that God made on the sixth day.

Our Paradoxical Nature

Before creating people, God made the land-animals. The waters brought forth the birds and fish, but cattle, creeping things, and beasts are of the earth. Cattle are herding creatures. They conform to each other and follow the leader. They are gregarious. They correspond to the conforming and gathering-together nature of the flesh. That's one of the reasons many people live in cities. It's part of their carnal nature. The natural instinct is even to follow the female leader. The oldest cow leads the herd. This maternal instinct is evident in some societies and even in some churches, but it shouldn't be where Jesus is Lord (see Rom. 12:2; 2 Cor. 10:12). God said:

> *As for My people, children are their oppressors, and* ***women rule over them****. O My people,* ***they which lead thee cause thee to err,*** *and destroy the way of thy paths* (Isaiah 3:12).

Proverbs 29:25 says, *"The fear of man bringeth a snare."* This is another aspect of people's cattle nature. It's not our fear of physical violence, but the fear of losing our honor that ensnares us. Saul lost his kingdom because of this weakness (see 1 Sam. 15:24). We can lose ours, too. Jesus said, *"Woe unto you, when all men shall speak well of you,"* (Luke 6:26) for, *"How can ye believe, which receive honor one of another, and seek not the honor that cometh from God only?"* (John 5:44). Jesus overcame this problem by making Himself of no reputation (see Phil. 2:7).

Creeping things also originate in the fleshly realm. One of the reasons satan has such an easy time deceiving people is their flesh is as deceitful as satan's spirit (see Eph. 4:14; 2 Tim. 3:6). Jeremiah said, *"The heart is deceitful above all things, and desperately wicked: who can know it?"* (Jer. 17:9). The Hebrew word translated *creep* means to glide smoothly, as when Jacob slicked his brother out of his blessing (see Gen. 27:18-36). Also, Jezebel operated in deception when she had Naboth slain (see 1 Kings 21:7-15). Cunning, crafty, deceitful, even charming or witchy—all are part of this side of humankind's paradoxical nature.

Then, there's the beastly nature of the flesh to deal with. Although not hard to interpret, often it's the hardest of all to overcome. Beastly people are dominating. They can be harsh and cruel as well. Stalin and Hitler both fall into this category. Sometimes pastors slip up and yield to this side of their fleshy nature, too. Churches ruled by beastly men are often factious sects or even cults (see 3 John 1:9).

The antichrist will exhibit all three of these natures at one time or another, but he *is* a beast. He is even called a beast in the Bible, and interestingly enough, his number is 666 (see Rev. 13:1-8).[2]

By examining these three carnal natures, the purpose of the sixth feast becomes obvious—judgment, and eternal judgment at that. In people's fallen condition, these natures are used to satisfy their selfish lusts. They're even used in their rebellion against their Creator. Every knee must bow, and every tongue must confess the lordship of Jesus Christ before God's work is finished on earth. *Then* He can rest.

We still have a job to do. *Six* means "image."[3] It often corresponds to the flesh, and as such, it is condemned and sentenced to die.

Endnotes

1. James Strong, *Strong's Exhaustive Concordance,* Hebrew #6754, 1823.
2. For more information on the meaning of the number 666, see Ira Milligan, *Understanding the Dreams You Dream, Vol. II* (Shippensburg, PA: Destiny Image, 2010), 25-26.
3. *Ibid,* 8-9.

DAY SEVEN

A PERFECT HEART

Thus the heavens and the earth were finished, and all the host of them. And on the seventh day God ended His work which He had made; and He rested on the seventh day from all His work which He had made. And God blessed the seventh day, and sanctified it: because that in it He had rested from all His work which God created and made (Genesis 2:1-3).

Seventh Column of Precepts

Feast of Tabernacles
Doctrine of Perfection
Baptism of Suffering (willing sacrifice)
The Sabbath rest

For the eyes of the Lord run to and fro throughout the whole earth, to shew Himself strong in the behalf of them whose heart is perfect toward Him... (2 Chronicles 16:9).

What is a perfect heart? Is there any such thing? Are there any perfect people in this day and time? Of course, Christ is perfect, and God made Christ (if anyone has a problem believing that Christ was *made*, notice the following Scripture):

But when the fullness of the time was come, God sent forth His Son, ***made*** *of a woman,* ***made*** *under the law* (Galatians 4:4).

After God finished His work (of making the perfect Man), He rested. His finished work is Christ. God's rest is called Sabbath. Paul said the Sabbath was a shadow, but the substance that made it was Christ:

Let no man therefore judge you in meat, or in drink, or in respect of an holyday, or of the new moon, or of the Sabbath days: Which are a shadow of things to come; but the body is of Christ (Colossians 2:16-17).

All things were made by Him; and without Him was not any thing made that was made. In Him was life; and the life was the light of men (John 1:3-4; see also Rev. 3:14, 21:6, 22:13).

Jesus is the Alpha and the Omega, the first and the last, the beginning and the end of the creation of God. Any attempt to interpret Scripture without Him is not only futile, it is heresy! Jesus *is* the Word of God. He is the Sabbath rest that God prepared for all humankind. That's the reason the Sabbath was part of the old covenant, and it *is* the new covenant:

Remember the Sabbath day, to keep it holy. Six days shalt thou labor, and do all thy work: But the seventh day is the Sabbath of the Lord thy God: in it thou shalt not do any work, thou, nor thy son, nor thy daughter, thy manservant, nor thy maidservant, nor thy cattle, nor thy stranger that is within thy gates: For in six days the Lord made heaven and earth, the sea, and all that in them is, and rested the seventh day: wherefore the Lord blessed the Sabbath day, and hallowed it (Exodus 20:8-11).

When a person attempts to earn God's acceptance through his own works, he defiles the Sabbath. When Christians rest in the finished work of the cross, they are keeping Sabbath. Moses' Law, holiness laws, religious trappings and traditions, anything and everything that replaces the cross offends God. One cannot conform to this (religious) world and still please God (see Rom. 12:2).

> *Ye shall keep the Sabbath therefore; for it is holy unto you:* ***every one that defiles it shall surely be put to death:*** *for whosoever does any work therein, that soul shall be cut off from among his people. Six days may work be done; but in the seventh is the Sabbath of rest, holy to the Lord:* ***whosoever does any work in the Sabbath day, he shall surely be put to death.*** *Wherefore the children of Israel shall keep the Sabbath, to observe the Sabbath throughout their generations,* ***for a perpetual covenant*** (Exodus 31:14-16).

We are saved by grace, through faith, alone (see Eph. 2:8). God purifies our hearts through faith, not works (see Acts 15:9). We are not saved by what we put *off*, but by what we put *on* (see 1 Pet. 3:21). Paul said, *"But put ye on the Lord Jesus Christ, and make not provision for the flesh, to fulfill the lusts thereof"* (Rom. 13:14).

Why must the image be put off at all? Because the perfect suit of His righteousness won't fit over it. It will only fit our spirits. We must discard the old, tattered garments of self-justification and self-righteousness and cover our sinful nakedness with the undergarment of humility before the immaculate suit of His perfect obedience will fit (see 1 Pet. 5:5). The old self's prideful, but vain attempts at obtaining righteousness must be offered as a willing sacrifice: Moses said, *"Thou shalt not let...a garment mingled of linen and woollen come upon thee"* [and John explained], *"for the fine linen is the righteousness of saints"* (Lev. 19:19; Rev. 19:8).

God requires His sheep to be sheared of their natural covering of works and self-righteousness and be clothed instead with His righteousness. He will not accept the two mingled together:

Christ is become of no effect unto you, whosoever of you are justified by the law; ye are fallen from grace (Galatians 5:4).

Have faith in God. Jesus said:

Let not your heart be troubled: ye believe in God, believe also in Me. In My Father's house are many mansions: if it were not so, I would have told you. I go to prepare a place for you. And if I go and prepare a place for you, I will come again, and receive you unto Myself; that where I am, there ye may be also (John 14:1-3).

A perfect heart is a heart filled with faith in God. A perfect person is one who through simple faith rests in Christ's finished work.

For thus saith the Lord God, the Holy One of Israel; in returning and rest shall ye be saved; in quietness and in confidence shall be your strength (Isaiah 30:15).

When Jesus therefore had received the vinegar, He said, ***It is finished***... (John 19:30).

Appendix A

Part II Questions

1. Is the description of the creation of people in the first chapter of Genesis literal or prophetic?
2. Why does Genesis chapter 2 describe Adam and Eve's creation if people were already created in chapter 1?
3. How is the information given in Genesis 1:1-5 illustrated (or interpreted) in the Gospel of John?
4. Some theologians believe that God made a race of people before Adam and Eve were created and later rejected them. What Scripture supports your opinion?
5. A. Why was Moses' Law given? B. What did it accomplish?
6. What are the four generations of the heavens and the earth?
7. Why is the millennium considered the time of God's rest?
8. Name the two primary divisions of the Word.
9. What is the difference between the *Logos* and a *rhema?*
10. A. The Bible says that God's natural creation teaches us spiritual truths (see Ps. 19:2-3; Rom. 1:20). Name at

least three spiritual parallels between Adam and Christ and two between Eve and the Church.

B. In nature, the strong survive and the weak perish. What Scriptures, if any, show this principle in Christians?

11. Does the sun teach us anything about the Son? If so, what?

12. What can we learn from an ant (see Prov. 6:6)?

13. A. What are the three natures of humanity?

    B. Are they good or bad?

    C. Give scriptural support for your answer.

Appendix B

Assignment Answers

LESSON ONE FIRST THE NATURAL, THEN THE SPIRITUAL

1. Show the spiritual meaning of Exodus 15:23-25:

> *So Moses brought Israel from the Red sea, and they went out into the wilderness of Shur; and they went three days in the wilderness, and found no water. And when they came to Marah, they could not drink of the waters of Marah, for they were bitter: therefore the name of it was called Marah. And the people murmured against Moses, saying, What shall we drink? And he cried unto the Lord; and the Lord showed him a tree, which when he had cast into the waters, the waters were made sweet: there he made for them a statute and an ordinance, and there he proved them* (Exodus 15:22-25).

The bitter waters of Marah represent the Law of Moses. The Law slew everyone who drank of it. The tree portrays Christ. Once He was "cut down," He became the Source of life to all who were under the curse of the Law. Even the "statute and an ordinance" points to the Law, which was shortly to be given by Moses.

2. Name the two primary divisions of the Word.

   The natural and the spiritual.

3. Which division corresponds to the Law, and which one corresponds to grace?

   The natural corresponds to the Law, and the spiritual corresponds to grace.

4. Which natural commandments and ordinances are we still required to obey?

   Only those agreed upon by the Jerusalem council listed in Acts 15:20.

   > *But that we write unto them, that they abstain from pollutions of idols, and from fornication, and from things strangled, and from blood* (Acts 15:20).

5. Has the whole Law been "done away with," as some teach?

   No, only the carnal commandments and ordinances (see Col. 2:14; Heb. 9:10).

6. A. What parts of the spirit of the Law are we supposed to keep? B. How?

   A. All of it. B. Through faith in God's promises and by the enablement of His grace (see Rom. 6:6-18; 2 Pet. 1:2-4).

ASSIGNMENT ANSWERS: LESSON TWO TYPES AND SHADOWS, NOT EXACT IMAGES

1. A. In Old Testament shadows, do women sometimes represent Christ? B. If so, why?

   A. Yes. B. Because submission is a feminine trait. When Christ humbled Himself and submitted Himself to the Father's will, in essence He took on Eve's role and became the Source (mother) of all living (see Gen. 3:20).

2. A. In shadows, do you think women may represent a specific role? B. If so, what?

   A. Yes. B. One role is the Church, the bride of Christ. Women may also represent witchcraft, as Jezebel does.

3. What is another name sometimes used for Old Testament shadows?

   Types.

4. A. Who does Benjamin represent? B. Explain why. C. Why do you think Joseph gave him five times more than his brethren (see Gen. 43:29-34)?

   A. The Church. B. Although Joseph and Benjamin were brothers, apparently Benjamin was still an infant when Joseph was sold into slavery, so they did not know each other. Likewise, Jesus and the saints are brothers who have never seen each other (we have not yet seen Jesus in the flesh). C. For the same reason that Joseph was given the silver cup—so that he would symbolize Christ's servants. *Five* means "serve or service." Eating is doing the will of God, as Christ did. Jesus wants us to work with Him in His Father's business.

   > *...he with whom it* [Joseph's silver cup] *is found shall be my servant; and ye shall be blameless* (Genesis 44:10).

   > *Jesus saith unto them, My meat is to do the will of Him that sent Me, and to finish His work* (John 4:34).

5. A. What does a beard symbolize? B. Although it was socially acceptable for men to wear beards in Joseph's day, he shaved when he was released from prison. Why?

A. A veil or covering. B. The face represents the heart. God's heart was covered with the Law. When Joseph came out of prison, it portrayed Jesus' resurrection. Christ's resurrection revealed God's heart. So when Joseph shaved, it represented the removal of the Law from God's heart, revealing *"the light of the knowledge of the glory of God in the face of Jesus Christ"* (2 Cor. 4:6).

6. Besides those we've discussed, name three more spiritual truths that we can learn from Joseph's life.

   He was given Pharaoh's signet ring, signifying the authority given Christ by the Father. Likewise, Christ received an eternal robe of righteousness and the gold chain speaks of eternal honor and glory as well.

ASSIGNMENT ANSWERS: LESSON THREE ALLEGORIES AND PARABLES

1. What is a parable?

   A simple story illustrating a moral or religious lesson.

2. A. Is Luke 16:19-31 a parable? B. How do you know one way or the other?

   A. Yes. B. Because He was speaking to the Pharisees (see Luke 16:14), and anytime He was speaking to a mixed group, He always used parables (see Matt. 13:34).

3. Explain Luke 6:47-49.

   > *Whosoever cometh to Me, and hears My sayings, and doeth them, I will shew you to whom he is like: He is like a man which built an house, and dug deep, and laid the foundation on a rock: and when the flood arose, the stream beat vehemently upon that house, and could not shake it: for it was*

> *founded upon a rock. But he that hears, and doeth not, is like a man that without a foundation built an house upon the earth; against which the stream did beat vehemently, and immediately it fell; and the ruin of that house was great* (Luke 6:47-49).

The rock is Christ, who is the Word of God. The house we build is our life. The floods and streams are the trials of life. When we live by faith in Christ and obey His Word, our lives are unshakable (see Heb. 12:26-28). The house built on earth is a life founded on the religious traditions and philosophies of people. Those teachings cannot prepare a person for the assault of life's problems. A life built on humanistic teachings will crumble.

4. What book of the Bible was specifically written to help unlock the mysteries hidden in parables?

   Proverbs.

5. A. What does divided hooves and animals chewing cuds have to do with walking in the Spirit? B. Swine have divided hooves. Why are they still considered unclean under Moses' Law?

   A. Divided hooves symbolize rightly dividing the Word, and cud chewing portrays meditating upon the Word. B. Because they don't chew the cud.

6. Why does God speak in parables? Why not just speak plainly?

   For two reasons. First, to give us the mysteries of the Kingdom. He uses parables to hide the truth from the wise and prudent, but He reveals them to those who seek Him. Second, so that He can be merciful unto all those who do not hear His word. By hiding the truth, He does not have to hold those who are ignorant of the truth accountable for their disobedience (see Rom. 11:32).

ASSIGNMENT ANSWERS: LESSON FOUR UNDERSTANDING SYMBOLS

1. Where did Jesus say that God hid the mysteries of the Kingdom?

   In parables (see Matt. 13:10-11,35).

2. What are the true riches of Luke 16:11?

   Wisdom, knowledge, and full assurance of understanding, i.e., faith (see Col. 2:2-3).

3. In Pharaoh's dream, how did Joseph know that cows meant prosperity?

   Because in the Egyptian culture, cattle meant wealth.

4. Does God still speak to us in dreams today?

   Yes! (See Acts 2:17.)

5. Name four ways that symbols acquire meaning.

   Inherent characteristics, personal experience, culture, and the Bible.

6. Which of the four is sometimes known as a symbol's universal meaning?

   Inherent characteristics.

ASSIGNMENT ANSWERS: LESSON FIVE EXAMPLES TO LIVE BY

1. A. What is the law of harvest? B. Is it still in effect? C. For how long?

   A. "*...whatsoever a man soweth, that shall he also reap*" (Gal. 6:7). B. Yes. C. For as long as the earth lasts (see Gen. 8:22).

2. Name three examples of the law of harvest operating in David's life. Explain what he reaped as a result of his actions in each of the examples you choose.

   He committed adultery, attempted to deceive Uriah, and then had him killed. As a result, his wives were defiled, his son deceived him, and then his two oldest sons were killed. He lost two-for-one in each case.

3. Is Paul's life a good example of the law of harvest? Explain your answer.

   Yes. Paul had Stephen stoned; then was stoned himself.

   > *I verily thought with myself, that I ought to do many things contrary to the name of Jesus of Nazareth. Which thing I also did in Jerusalem: and many of the saints did I shut up in prison, having received authority from the chief priests; and when they were put to death, I gave my voice against them. And I punished them oft in every synagogue, and compelled them to blaspheme; and being exceedingly mad against them, I persecuted them even unto strange cities* (Acts 26:9-11).

   > *And the multitude rose up together against them [Paul and Silas]: and the magistrates rent off their clothes, and commanded to beat them. And when they had laid many stripes upon them, they cast them into prison, charging the jailer to keep them safely: Who, having received such a charge, thrust them into the inner prison, and made their feet fast in the stocks* (Acts 16:22-24).

4. A. Under similar circumstances, would Daniel's response to the king's commandment in Daniel 6:7-10 still be the right thing to do today? Give Scripture to support your answer. B. How do you reconcile your answer with First Peter 2:13-16?

   A. Yes.

> *Then Peter and the other apostles answered and said, We ought to obey God rather than men* (Acts 5:29).

B. We're supposed to obey the higher authority, and God's commands are always higher than people's (see Rom. 13:1).

5. As God's ministers, are our lives supposed to be examples also? Give at least two Scriptures to support your answer.

   Yes.

   > *Let no man despise thy youth; but **be thou an example of the believers,** in word, in conversation, in charity, in spirit, in faith, in purity* (1 Timothy 4:12).

   > *In all things **showing thyself a pattern of good works:** in doctrine showing incorruptness, gravity, sincerity, sound speech, that cannot be condemned; that he that is of the contrary part may be ashamed, having no evil thing to say of you* (Titus 2:7-8).

   > *Remember them which have the rule over you, who have spoken unto you the word of God: **whose faith follow, considering the end of their conversation*** (Hebrews 13:7).

6. A. What is the second division of the Word? B. What does it reveal?

   A. The division of the soul from the spirit. B. The separation of the conscious mind from the conscience. It also corresponds to Christ and the Church.

ASSIGNMENT ANSWERS: LESSON SIX
GREAT PLAINNESS OF SPEECH

1. Does the Genesis 3:16 curse of women bringing forth children in sorrow still apply today?

Yes; all Old Testament curses are perpetual. They apply to everyone born, throughout all history, except for those who have obeyed the Gospel and are covered by the blood of Jesus (see Gal. 3:10).

2. A. What conditions must a couple meet before they can claim the promise of First Timothy 2:14-15? B. Can a woman's husband hinder her from obtaining the promise?

   A. They must continue in faith and charity and holiness with sobriety. B. Yes.

3. A. What did Noah's flood represent? B. Was the flood literal or figurative?

   A. The Law of Moses. B. Both.

4. Was God vengeful or redemptive when He destroyed the earth with the flood?

   Redemptive. If God had not stopped the advancement of wickedness, humankind would have eventually destroyed itself.

5. A. Is the fire that Peter said will melt the elements with fervent heat literal, or is Peter speaking figuratively? B. How do you know?

   A. Literal. B. Because it is in the "great plainness of speech" Scriptures.

6. Why would God burn up the earth?

   To purge it of wickedness. If He doesn't, humankind will annihilate itself.

   > *And except those days should be shortened, there should no flesh be saved: but for the elect's sake those days shall be shortened* (Matthew 24:22).

And the nations were angry, and Thy wrath is come, and the time of the dead, that they should be judged, and that thou shouldest give reward unto thy servants the prophets, and to the saints, and them that fear Thy name, small and great; and shouldest destroy them which destroy the earth (Revelation 11:18).

ASSIGNMENT ANSWERS: LESSON SEVEN TWO OR THREE WITNESSES

1. How many different scriptural witnesses (writers) should one have before any specific doctrine is accepted as correct?

   At least two.

2. Does the rule of two or more witnesses apply to the *rhema* word too?

   Yes (see 1 Cor. 13:1).

3. Why is this rule important?

   It helps protect us from error, both in interpreting Scripture, and in personal guidance as we follow God.

4. How do we obey Paul's command to *"prove all things"*?

   Search the Scriptures to learn and compare everything that God said about any given subject, not accepting any one person's explanation or doctrine without searching it out.

5. Many people believe that one third of the angels fell along with satan when he fell from Heaven. Are there any Scriptures that support this doctrine?

   No, there are none. No one knows exactly how many angels fell. The Bible simply tells us that Jesus saw him fall.

And He [Jesus] said unto them, I beheld Satan as lightning fall from heaven (Luke 10:18).

6. A. Why do you believe what you believe? Is it because you have *"proved all things, and you are holding fast to that which is good"?* (1 Thess. 5:21). If not, what should you do?

   A. Correct reason: "Because I've searched it out." The most common reason: "I believe what I've been taught." If you have *"proved all things,"* that's good; but if not, of course, start searching it out today.

ASSIGNMENT ANSWERS: LESSON EIGHT DISTINCT, EXACT, AND PRECISELY ON TIME

1. A. In Lesson Seven, the question was raised about how many angels fell with satan. If Revelation 12:3-4 is used to support the age-old belief that one third of the angels fell with him, does Revelation 1:1 agree with that interpretation? B. Why, or why not?

   A. No. B. Because satan fell into sin in the Garden of Eden (see Gen. 3:1-5; John 8:44). What John saw and recorded wasn't to happen until after John's day.

2. A. What is the real meaning of Revelation 12:3-4? B. When will it occur?

   A. The stars represent God's ministers (see Dan. 12:3). The dragon probably represents satan operating in and through the antichrist. If so, his tail is the false prophet (see Isaiah 9:15).

   And they that understand among the people shall instruct many: yet they shall fall by the sword, and by flame, by captivity, and by spoil, many days....And some of them of understanding shall fall, to try them, and to purge, and to make them white, even to the time of the end: because it is yet for a time appointed (Daniel 11:33-35).

B. Probably at the time of the mark of the beast, before Christ returns.

3. What three questions should we ask about each Scripture before we finalize our interpretation of it?

   What did God actually say? What did He *mean*? *Why* did He say what He said?

4. A. When will the rapture occur? B. What are some of the signs that Jesus said we will see before He returns? C. Are any of these signs visible now?

   A. After the great tribulation is over. B. The great tribulation is one. Also, great distress upon nations, earthquakes, famines, wars, the mark of the beast, etc. C. Yes, great distress, fear, pestilence (AIDS), increase in the number of earthquakes, etc.

5. A. Jesus said that no one will know the *"day nor the hour"* of His return (Matt. 25:13). Does that mean we can't know anything at all about the timing of His return? B. What did Paul say about this doctrine?

   A. No.

   B. *But of the times and the seasons, brethren, ye have no need that I write unto you. For yourselves know perfectly that the day of the Lord so cometh as a thief in the night. For when they shall say, Peace and safety; then sudden destruction cometh upon them, as travail upon a woman with child; and they shall not escape. But ye, brethren, are not in darkness, that that day should overtake you as a thief* (1 Thessalonians 5:1-4).

6. A. Do you think Jesus could come back right now? Tonight? B. Why, or why not?

   A. No. B. Because the Word says:

   > *And He shall send Jesus Christ, which before was preached unto you: Whom the heaven must receive* ***until*** *the times of restitution of all things, which God hath spoken by the mouth of all His holy prophets since the world began* (Acts 3:20-21).

   > *Now we beseech you, brethren, by the coming of our Lord Jesus Christ, and by our gathering together unto him, that ye be not soon shaken in mind, or be troubled, neither by spirit, nor by word, nor by letter as from us, as that the day of Christ is at hand. Let no man deceive you by any means:* ***for that day shall not come, except there come a falling away first, and that man of sin be revealed, the son of perdition*** (2 Thessalonians 2:1-3).

ASSIGNMENT ANSWERS: LESSON NINE LINE UPON LINE, PRECEPT UPON PRECEPT

1. A. What, more than anything else, blocks our understanding of "new" truth? B. Does this hindrance come from our souls or from our spirits? C. How do you know?

   A. Our pride. B. From our spirits. C. Because the pride of life is an attribute of our spirits.

2. A. Which one of our wills is acceptable with God, our flesh's will, our souls', or our spirits'? B. Give at least one Scripture to prove that your answer is correct.

   A. Only the will of our spirits (see Matt. 26:41).

B. *But as many as received Him, to them gave He power to become the sons of God, even to them that believe on His name: Which were born, not of blood, nor of the will of the flesh, nor of the will of man [soul], but of God* (John 1:12-13).

3. What other Scriptures can you think of that could be made into a grid like the Hebrews 4:12 grid that we studied?

   There are many. Although all of them don't apply, the time chart lists several that fall into place properly if number 20 is placed first:

   For I delivered unto you first of all that which I also received, how that Christ died for our sins according to the scriptures; and that He was buried, and that He rose again the third day according to the scriptures (1 Corinthians 15:3-4).

4. A. Is covetousness a matter of fleshly lust or lust that proceeds forth from one's soul? B. Is covetousness ever acceptable with God?

   A. Covetousness is from the soul (for that reason, it can be good or evil). B. Yes. We are supposed to covet things above (see Col. 3:2).

   But covet earnestly the best gifts: and yet shew I unto you a more excellent way (1 Corinthians 12:31).

   Wherefore, brethren, covet to prophesy, and forbid not to speak with tongues (1 Corinthians 14:39).

5. A. Why is it natural for people to desire others to envy them? B. Is this acceptable with God?

   A. Because we are created in God's likeness, and God desires worship. B. No!

6. A. Great athletes and movie stars have fans. Is it all right to be one of those fans, or is it wrong? B. Why?

   A. No. B.

   Then saith Jesus unto him, Get thee hence, Satan: for it is written, Thou shalt worship the Lord thy God, and Him only shalt thou serve (Matthew 4:10).

ASSIGNMENT ANSWERS: LESSON TEN FOR MATURE CHRISTIANS ONLY

1. From memory, list five or more important things one should consider as he or she divides the Word of God.

   (1) Divide the natural from the spiritual (2) Interpret and use the information contained in types, shadows, allegories, and parables (3) Always allow the Word to interpret its own symbols (4) Live by the natural examples and patterns (5) Interpret each Scripture within its own context (6) Observe the "great plainness of speech" rule (never spiritualize anything that the apostles have already spiritualized) (7) Establish every Word with at least two different witnesses (8) Observe God's timing when interpreting His Word (9) Put line on line, and precept upon precept.

2. A. How many times a year were the Jews supposed to gather together before the Lord? B. What were they gathering for?

   A. Three times a year. B. To celebrate the seven feasts.

3. A. What is the significance of the feast of Unleavened Bread? B. Why did it last seven days?

   A. It is symbolic of cleansing oneself of sin. B. *Seven* means "complete or all." We are to search until we are completely free of wrong thoughts, words, and deeds, including wrong attitudes, lusts, bondage, and all other sinful activity.

4. A. How many days from the feast of firstfruits were the Israelites supposed to count before starting the next feast? B. What was this next feast called?

   A. Forty-nine. The next one started on the fiftieth day. B. The feast of Pentecost.

5. A. Is there another line of seven precepts that we could put with the two we used? B. What Scripture is it? C. Would it give us additional information if we did?

   A. Yes. B. Genesis 1:1-2:2. C. Yes, a lot!

6. A. Are we still supposed to keep the Jewish feasts? B. Why, or why not?

   A. Yes and no. We're *not* obligated to keep them in the natural, but we *must* keep them in the spirit.

   > ***Therefore let us keep the feast****, not with old leaven, neither with the leaven of malice and wickedness; but with the unleavened bread of sincerity and truth* (1 Corinthians 5:8).

   B. *Naturally*, they were all fulfilled in the death, burial, resurrection, and the witness of the resurrection of Christ. But, if we don't keep the *spiritual* feasts of Passover and Unleavened Bread, we cannot even be saved. Then, the spiritual fulfillment of the feasts of firstfruits and Pentecost separates us from the Law and empowers us to be witnesses of Christ's resurrection. Likewise, the spiritual fulfillment of the feasts of trumpets, atonement, and tabernacles brings us into unity, love, and maturity and equips us for the work of the ministry.

ASSIGNMENT ANSWERS: LESSON ELEVEN NO OTHER FOUNDATION

1. A. How many different baptisms are there? B. Name them.

   A. Seven B. Repentance, faith, water, Spirit, fire (power), fire (purification), suffering.

2. Which baptism saves us?

   Faith.

3. A. Why should we be water baptized? B. What does water baptism accomplish in a believer's life?

   A. To fulfill all righteousness. B. It removes us from under the natural ordinances of Moses' Law.

4. What is the proper way to baptize someone? B. Who is authorized to perform water baptism?

   A. By immersing them in water in the name of the Lord Jesus Christ (see Acts 2:38; 8:38; 10:48; 19:5; Col. 3:17). B. Any and all believers (see Mark 16:15-18).

5. A. Name three things the Holy Spirit baptism accomplishes in a believer's life. B. What else does the Bible call the Holy Spirit?

   A. Guides them into all truth; shows them things to come and brings all things into their remembrance whatsoever God has said to them. B. The Comforter, and the Spirit of truth, holiness, adoption, wisdom, revelation, and grace.

6. A. Which baptism is common to two different feasts and accomplishes two different things? B. What are they?

   A. The baptism of fire. B. Power and purification.

ASSIGNMENT ANSWERS: LESSON TWELVE MAGNIFY THE LAW

1. What does it mean to "magnify the Law"?

   Reveal its spiritual meaning.

2. What do the Scriptures compare hatred for one's brother to?

   Murder (see 1 John 3:15).

3. Is looking at pornography adultery? B. Why?

   A. Yes. B.

   > *But I say unto you, That whosoever looketh on a woman to lust after her hath committed adultery with her already in his heart* (Matthew 5:28).

4. A. What happens to people who do not honor their parents? B. Is dishonoring parents a violation of the old covenant or the new?

   A. They have problems in the same area that they dishonor their parents in. For example, if they judge their father because he is a poor provider, they will have problems providing for their family. B. The New. Christians who have obeyed the Gospel are free from the old covenant through Christ's blood.

5. A. Which day is a Christian's Sabbath day? B. Are Christians required to keep the Jewish Sabbath? C. Why, or why not?

   A. Every day is Sabbath. We rest in the finished work of Christ. B. No. It is part of the old covenant. C. For the same reason that we don't have to keep any of the other carnal ordinances and commandments; Jesus fulfilled and satisfied them all.

6. Under what condition would it be a sin for a Christian to refrain from working in order to keep Sabbath?

   If he does so as a requirement for his salvation.

APPENDIX C

PART II ANSWERS

1. Is the description of the creation of man in the first chapter of Genesis literal or prophetic?

   Both. Adam was the first man created, and he was *"the figure of Him that was to come"* (Rom. 5:14; 1 Cor. 15:45). Likewise, Eve was the first woman, and she is a type of the Church (see Eph. 5:23-25, 31-32).

2. Why does Genesis chapter 2 describe Adam and Eve's creation if people were already created in chapter 1?

   Because chapter 1 is God's prophetic blueprint, declaring His plan of creation and redemption before it was actually done. Chapter 2 is the beginning of the literal record of His works.

3. How is the information given in Genesis 1:1-5 illustrated (or interpreted) in the Gospel of John?

   > *In the beginning was the Word, and the Word was with God, and the Word was God. The same was in the beginning with God. All things were made by Him; and without Him was not any thing made that was made. In*

Him was life; and the life was the light of men. And the light shined in darkness; and the darkness comprehended it not (John 1:1-5).

4. A. Some theologians believe that God made a race of people before Adam and Eve were created and later rejected them. Then He created Adam and Eve to repopulate the earth. Is this doctrine correct? B. What Scripture supports your opinion?

   A. No, because God said Adam was the first man.

   B. *And so it is written, The* ***first man*** *Adam was made a living soul; the last Adam was made a quickening spirit. The* ***first man*** *is of the earth, earthy: the second Man is the Lord from heaven* (1 Corinthians 15:45,47).

5. A. Why was Moses' Law given? B. What did it accomplish?

   A. It was given for several different reasons. The first was to bring people into accountability for their sin (see Rom. 5:13). The second was to bring people to Christ (see Gal. 3:24). A third was to establish the principal of substitutionary offerings for sin (see Lev. 4:13-20). A fourth was to establish justification by faith (see Hab. 2:4; Gal. 3:6).

   B. It accomplished all four, but by making people accountable for their sin, it also destroyed them.

6. What are the four generations of the heavens and the earth?

   Innocence, Law, Grace, and Millennium (Rewards).

7. Why is the millennium considered the time of God's rest?

   Because the Church will be complete (finished) and satan will be bound for a thousand years.

8. Name the two primary divisions of the Word and three different levels of interpretation.

   Natural division (corresponding to the historical or body level of interpretation), Spiritual division (corresponding to the Christological—spirit level), and Prophetic division (soul level of interpretation).

9. What is the difference between the *Logos* and a *rhema?*

   The written Word of God (Scripture) is usually referred to as the *Logos* (a thought that has been expressed). John said that Jesus is the *Logos* (the living Word). A *rhema* (a thought that is currently being expressed) refers to a word of prophecy, including dreams and visions, when they are from God.

10. The Bible says that God's natural creation teaches us spiritual truths (see Ps. 19:2-3; Rom. 1:20). Name at least three spiritual parallels between Adam and Christ and two between Eve and the Church.

    Adam was God's son; he was given authority over all of God's creation; his bride was taken out of his side; he died willingly for his bride's sake; by his death, all people die. By Christ's resurrection, all people are resurrected. Eve was the bride of God's son; she was taken out of his side; she was the mother of all living.

11. In nature, the strong survive and the weak perish. What Scriptures (Old or New Testament), if any, show this principle in Christians?

    > *Finally, my brethren, be strong in the Lord, and in the power of His might. Put on the whole armor of God, that ye may be able to stand against the wiles of the devil* (Eph. 6:10-11; also see 1 Sam. 15:2; Isa. 53:12; 1 Pet. 5:8).

12. Does the sun teach us anything about the Son? If so, what?

    Yes. Jesus is the light of the world (see John 9:5); both the sun and the Son rule over the day (see Ps. 89:36); Jesus rose out of darkness (see Mal. 4:2); the sun is impartial, ministering equally to good and bad, and the Son is good to the just and the unjust (see Matt. 5:45; Ps. 84:11).

13. What can we learn from an ant (see Prov. 6:6)?

    Team work; proper work ethics; the value of sharing; examples of proper spiritual warfare; principal of preparing for the future (hard times, etc.).

14. A. What are the three natures of humankind? B. Are they good or bad? C. Give scriptural support for your answer.

    A. Conform, wisdom, and dominion. B. Good, unless used selfishly. C. Genesis 1:31; Matthew 12:35.

About Ira Milligan

Ira and Judy Milligan have served God since 1962. In 1986 they founded Servant Ministries, Inc. They travel and Ira teaches and presents such seminars including: Dreams and Their Interpretation; Prophets and Personal Prophecy; Counseling and Deliverance; Personal Spiritual Warfare, and Rediscovering the New Testament Church. Both Ira and his wife minister in the gifts of the Spirit, and Judy ministers in music.

Ira is the author of several books, including the popular *Understanding the Dreams You Dream* and *The Master's Voice—A Practical Guide to Personal Ministry.* He has taught classes on counseling as a guest lecturer at Oral Roberts University.

Ira and his wife reside in Tioga, Louisiana. They have four children and eleven grandchildren.

For information about seminars conducted in your church, write or email:

Servant Ministries Inc.
PO Box 1120
Tioga, LA 71477
Email: servantministries@suddenlink.net
Web page: www.servant-ministries.org

Other Books by Ira Milligan

The Hidden Power of Covenant

Releasing the Fullness of the Blessing of the Gospel

Hidden Mysteries of the Bible, Vol. I

52 Lesson Foundational Bible Study Course

Hidden Mysteries of the Bible, Vol. II

52 Lesson Advanced Bible Study Course

Truth or Consequences

The Truth Will Make You Free

The Master's Voice

A Guide to Personal Ministry

Euroclydon

Illustrating the Four Winds

In the right hands, This Book will Change Lives!

Most of the people who need this message will not be looking for this book. To change their lives, you need to put a copy of this book in their hands.

> *But others (seeds) fell into good ground, and brought forth fruit, some a hundred-fold, some sixty-fold, some thirty-fold* (Matthew 13:8).

Our ministry is constantly seeking methods to find the good ground, the people who need this anointed message to change their lives. Will you help us reach these people?

> *Remember this—a farmer who plants only a few seeds will get a small crop. But the one who plants generously will get a generous crop* (2 Corinthians 9:6).

EXTEND THIS MINISTRY BY SOWING
3 BOOKS, 5 BOOKS, 10 BOOKS, **OR MORE TODAY**,
AND BECOME A LIFE CHANGER!

Thank you,

Don Nori Sr., Founder
Destiny Image
Since 1982